HOW TO SURVIVE IN
ANGLO-SAXON
ENGLAND

To all the custodians and volunteers at the venues we visited
across England in search of information and images for this book.
Thank you to everyone for your generosity and help.
This work could not exist without you.

HOW TO SURVIVE IN
ANGLO-SAXON
ENGLAND

TONI MOUNT

PEN & SWORD
HISTORY

AN IMPRINT OF PEN & SWORD BOOKS LTD.
YORKSHIRE - PHILADELPHIA

First published in Great Britain in 2024 by
PEN AND SWORD HISTORY
An imprint of
Pen & Sword Books Ltd
Yorkshire – Philadelphia

Copyright © Toni Mount, 2024

ISBN 978 1 39905 573 4

Typeset in Times New Roman 12/16 by
SJmagic DESIGN SERVICES, India.
Printed and bound in the UK by CPI Group (UK) Ltd.

Pen & Sword Books Limited incorporates the imprints of Atlas, Archaeology,
Aviation, Discovery, Family History, Fiction, History, Maritime, Military,
Military Classics, Politics, Select, Transport, True Crime, Air World, Frontline
Publishing, Leo Cooper, Remember When, Seaforth Publishing, The Praetorian
Press, Wharncliffe Local History, Wharncliffe Transport, Wharncliffe True Crime
and White Owl.

For a complete list of Pen & Sword titles please contact
PEN & SWORD BOOKS LIMITED
George House, Units 12 & 13, Beevor Street, Off Pontefract Road,
Barnsley, South Yorkshire, S71 1HN, England
E-mail: enquiries@pen-and-sword.co.uk
Website: www.pen-and-sword.co.uk

or

PEN AND SWORD BOOKS
1950 Lawrence Rd, Havertown, PA 19083, USA
E-mail: uspen-and-sword@casematepublishers.com
Website: www.penandswordbooks.com

Contents

Contents

Chapter 1

Introduction

Have you read *The Lord of the Rings* trilogy or *The Hobbit?* These wonderful tales were written by J. R. R. Tolkien, the Rawlinson and Bosworth Professor of Anglo-Saxon – the language of Old English – at Oxford University between 1925 and 1945. Written for his children, these stories and a series of sequels created an entire fantasy world based on Tolkien's vast knowledge of the Anglo-Saxon language and literature. If you haven't read the books, you may have been captivated by the movies based upon them, whisking you away to a land where elves, dwarves, hobbits and men battle wicked wizards, orcs and dragons, in search of enchanted rings, magic swords and a happy ending.

But supposing you could travel through time, back to those dark days, what is life in Anglo-Saxon England really like? Is life as dangerous as Tolkien's books describe? How would you survive among people who believe elves and dragons exist and may disrupt your daily existence upon a whim? How might you keep safe when warriors clash, as pagans become Christians and then change their minds again?

So much changes during the six centuries when the Germanic Anglo-Saxons rule this country. Not only do the people become Christian, eventually forsaking their old gods, but society becomes literate, recording literature and law in written documents. Ideas of government and a legal code lay the foundations for our own time. The Anglo-Saxons even give us the days of the week. Coinage is increasingly important for trade, rather than just bartering one commodity for another. But not everything is an 'improvement': the fabulously crafted jewellery of early days becomes less evident; the gap between the wealthy and the poor widens.

This book is a guide to help you survive in those perilous times, should you choose to travel back. It will advise you on how to behave, how to speak – or when to keep quiet – mealtimes, religion and entertaining the friends you make. Also, it suggests the best ways to avoid Viking raiders and diseases. What should you do if you're unlucky and fall sick? What happens if you get in trouble with the law?

This set of handy hints will help you to get the best out of your visit and enjoy your adventure in Anglo-Saxon England.

Setting the Scene

In AD 410, the Romans who had ruled this country for almost four centuries withdrew and the last legions departed Britannia. The Roman Empire was being attacked by barbarian hordes on all sides and the wealthiest parts further east were under threat of being overrun. Britain, being a poorer, distant outpost, was told to fend for itself and look to its own defence while the army hurried to protect Rome's heartlands. Britain was expendable. The legions left behind a multicultural society of Celts – the original inhabitants of these islands – people from across the Roman Empire who had made their homes here and more recent incomers. Among these last were Angles, Saxons, Jutes, Frisians and other Germanic folk from Northern Europe who had never experienced direct Roman rule.

There was bound to be a bit of a culture clash. Whereas Roman Britain had been Christian – nominally, at least – with a monetary economy, a civil service, a unified legal system, towns and cities, the newcomers were pagan, traded by barter, had no overall government or legislation and were used to living as small, farming and fishing communities. Even their military capabilities were based on leadership of the moment with strong men commanding an assemblage of volunteer warriors until the situation no longer required them.

Unfortunately for us, something else the Romans had, which these Germanic people did not, was literacy. Most of what little we know of the early decades of fifth-century Britain comes from 'foreign' writers so we don't have the inside story. No wonder historians used to call this period 'the Dark Ages'. But just how dark were the Dark Ages? What do we know of the Germanic tribes? Why did these migrants come in the first place and then decide to stay and make this their home?

Although there is little historic certainty about any of this, it seems most likely that Angles, Saxons, Jutes and Frisians were known here before the Romans left, probably through peaceful trading because we know their ships were suited to sea-going voyages and they had skill in navigation. Surprisingly, their ships were described as being stitched from hides – that is leather over a wooden framework. Also, during the later fourth century, Pictish tribesmen from the north of Hadrian's Wall, Scots (confusingly, from Ireland) and other invaders were causing problems for the reduced Roman garrisons and mercenaries were invited to help out with the promise of reward for services rendered. It's thought that Germanic warriors were among those eager to oblige. Once the Roman army left, taking the civil servants, Christian priests and officials with them, matters seem to have deteriorated quite rapidly. Another problem was that any fit, young British men would have been seconded as auxiliaries and forced to leave with the legions to defend more important parts of the empire, so few, if any, warriors remained in Britain and Roman law had forbidden civilians from carrying weapons.

Undefended and without any infrastructure for raising or training a militia, Britain was a ripe plum for the picking, tempting any would-be invader to take the chance. At some point, a king was chosen, elected or simply put himself forward as a leader. The Venerable Bede, writing centuries later, calls him 'Vortigern' but that is a title – something like 'High King', rather than a name. To Vortigern and his council, it probably seemed the obvious and sensible thing to do: around AD 430, the Saxon mercenary allies were asked to bring in more of their fellows from home to drive out the Picts and Scots.

The foreign sources tend to refer to them as 'Saxons' although they could have been a mix of Germanic peoples. It seems a contingent of Jutish warriors were the first to arrive on the Isle of Thanet off the north-east coast of Kent, possibly led by two brothers, Hengist and Horsa, who may be more legendary than real. All went as planned, the invaders were driven back north and the time came for the mercenaries to be paid off and return home. Whether the reward wasn't considered generous enough – it seems that land was given as part of the prize – or because the mercenaries had come to love the fertile country they fought so hard to defend, the 'Saxons' refused to leave and turned on their paymasters, seizing control of parts of Britain around AD 440 or 441.

But they didn't have it all their own way. A new generation of Britons was growing up without the benefits of a paid army to defend them and they were learning the arts of war out of necessity. A leader, Ambrosius Aurelianus, probably a well-born Romano-Briton, gathered an army to fight the Saxons and they clashed in a great battle at Mount Badon, though no one has been able to identify this site. The Britons were victorious, taking back parts of the country and – so the chronicler, Gildas, tells us when he wrote his *The Ruin of Britain* in the 540s – the Saxons went home. He says this happened around AD 500 but he isn't very good with dates and it could have been earlier but probably not later or he would have known people who remembered the event. But, as time-travellers, we can ask the man himself:

'God give you good day, Ambrosius Aurelianus. May we ask you about the problems you are having with the Saxons?'

'I'm preparing to do battle with these accursed pagans this very day, so I can't waste time on questions. I must arm and beseech God's blessings upon our endeavours.'

'Don't worry: you'll be victorious, this time, at least.'

'Are you a sooth-sayer? A prophet?'

'Trust me on this. I can also tell you that your exploits will become the stuff of legend.'

'And rightly so. The name of Ambrosius Aurelianus should be known to our children and our children's children and our children's children's children…'

'Yes, yes, don't go on. But I'm afraid you will not be known to posterity as Ambrosius Aurelianus. They will call you King Arthur.'

'Who? Are you saying my illustrious name will be forgotten?'

'I'm afraid so.'

'But that's terrible. Why should I bother fighting these Saxons if no one will remember me? I may as well lose this battle and just die with honour.'

'You can't do that. Your success today is foretold in, er, all the books that will be written.'

'But you say they'll call me Arthur? Why can't they get my name right?'

'Even the Saxons will remember you and people a thousand years in the future and more will write about you and think you're marvellous, enjoying your adventures.'

'Mm, maybe that's not so bad. 'Arthur', you say?'

'It means strong as a bear or bear-hero in Welsh. I checked it out with google.'

'Is he another sooth-sayer?'

'Sort of. A fount of all knowledge, anyway.'

'A pagan deity! Only God knows everything. Go away, you demon. I'll not listen to your barbarian prattle. Be off, I say.'

That didn't go as I'd hoped but it is thought by some scholars that Ambrosius Aurelianus could be the original King Arthur, the great war-leader or Dux Bellorum, who did battle with the Saxons and won. Maybe after that defeat, some Saxons did go back to the Continent or perhaps they simply withdrew to particular areas of the country still under their control. Whatever the true situation, from c.430, Germanic archaeology appears in Britain – non-Christian funeral practices, grave goods, etc. – and it's here to stay, as are the Saxons themselves.

Who are the Anglo-Saxon people?

The Venerable Bede, a Northumbrian monk writing in AD 731, tells us the origins of the newcomers and where they chose to settle in their adopted land. Archaeological evidence supports his story quite closely, although not exactly. This is what Bede says of the settlement of these peoples:

> The Jutes [from Jutland on the Danish peninsula] settled in Kent in SE England, the Isle of Wight just off the south coast and on the mainland opposite the island [Hampshire]. From Old Saxony [northern Germany] came the East Saxons who settled in Essex, the South Saxons who made their home in Sussex to the west of Kent and the West Saxons who occupied much of Hampshire, Wiltshire, Dorset and the Thames Valley and the Middle Saxons in Middlesex, close to London. The Angles, Bede continues, who came from Angulus

Anglo-Saxon carving of three saints in St Mary & St Hardulph Church, Breedon-on-the-Hill, Leics.

[today Angeln] in southern Denmark, between the Jutish and Saxon kingdoms, took over East Anglia, Mercia [the Midlands] and Northumbria north of the River Humber. So many Angles left their homeland that he reports 'Angulus is said to have remained deserted from that day to this'.

And recent archaeology done in Angeln in Schleswig confirms abandoned villages from 450 onwards.

Although Bede doesn't mention them, the Frisians from the Netherlands were also leaving their coastal homes and farms to come to Britain in search of a new life. Again, archaeology reveals that these clear-cut divisions of where each tribe settled isn't entirely true. For example, Saxon brooches are found from Yorkshire to Hampshire and all the eastern counties in between. In reality, crossing the North Sea seems to have blurred the distinctions to some extent. This wasn't unexpected because the tribes shared a common language, a common religion and some traditions.

Why did they leave their homelands?

The new people weren't only warriors, although adventurous young men were undoubtedly the first to arrive. Eventually, these men brought their families, livestock, farming and fishing tools, intending to stay, build homes and communities and make a fresh start. Historians aren't certain why and there are a number of suggestions. One possible reason was those same barbarian hordes threatening the Roman Empire. A great influx of people from the east wasn't just pressurising the Romans. Their westward expansion was pushing the Germanic tribes farther and farther west and north and for those on the northern coasts of Europe, they were running out of land. It didn't help that, then as now, global warming was causing sea levels to rise significantly, pushing those same people inland, away from the coasts, narrowing the area available to them on which to farm, fish and so feed the population. They were in an increasingly impossible situation and relocation to a wide, fertile land, inhabited by unwarlike, disorganised Christians must have been an easy choice for the desperate, overcrowded Saxons and their kind.

Living together

Whatever really happened after the battle of Mount Badon, wherever it happened or when, there is still much academic argument as to what became of the victors that day. History tells us that Britain became England, ruled by the incomers, speaking English, so where were the Romano-British, the Celts? Some say they were slaughtered *en masse* by the Saxons and the survivors fled westwards and northwards, to Cornwall, Wales and Scotland – Celtic outposts even in the twenty-first century with their own versions of the Celtic languages and traditions. That must be how it was because our modern English language contains barely a word of Celtic – or Common Brittonic or Brythonic to give it its official name – so it must have been wiped out with those who spoke it. Yet there is little archaeological evidence either for killing on an appalling scale or a great exodus to the west. In fact, place names and DNA analysis tell a different story.

In my own humble opinion – allowing for localised skirmishes and blood-letting – on the whole the Saxons, Angles, Jutes, etc. settled down in their own villages often close to but separate from their Celtic neighbours. This is evident from place names. Although there is a great deal of scholarly argument about the name and its original meaning, London had Celtic roots before the Romans came and Latinised it to Londinium. Some rivers in south east England have also kept their Celtic names: most notably the Thames; the Fleet – of which there are a number – is fast-flowing; Lea is a bright, sparkling river; the Stour flows strongly. The ranges of chalk hills known as the North and South Downs derive their name from 'don', a Celtic word for hill. Croydon means crow hill, for example, but East Kent boasts

---

Did You Know?

The word 'glas' from which we derive 'glass' is a Celtic word meaning blue, or blue-grey or the green of natural things, or the colour of water or even day-break. But 'glas' is also an Old English word meaning shiny or glossy. Did the French borrow this word to describe ice – glacé? In the past, early glass was always greenish in tint and rarely clear, so the Celtic 'glas' would describe it perfectly, as would the OE word describe its shiny surface reflecting the light. So modern English may have more hidden Celtic words than we realise.

Harbledown, Kingsdown and The Downs near Deal. A Celtic word for valley is 'combe', common in Cornwall and Devon but it remains in the Kentish place names Swanscombe and Ulcombe. Blean, near Canterbury, means 'upland' in Celtic. Why would the Saxons keep these old names unless they were still outnumbered by the native speakers referring to the rivers, hills and valleys in their own language? Another place name, Walton, so common across England, from Surrey to Cumbria, from Essex to Dorset, is Old English for 'farm or hamlet of the Welsh' – in other words the Celtic speakers.

The other subject I mentioned is DNA. The analysis of DNA is a more recent tool in the historian's kit and is beginning to reveal more about the genetics of those who live on these islands. However, being a relatively new field of study, there is much more to do and results so far are often debatable, confusing and probably inaccurate. Gleaned from various sources, it seems the average modern Briton has between 40% and 75% Anglo-Saxon DNA, depending on how far north and west the samples were taken. To the east and south the percentage is higher. But when the X chromosome [female line of decent] is compared to the Y chromosome [male line of decent] we get a different story: X has far less Anglo-Saxon heritage than Y. This tells us that those mercenary Germanic warriors took many Celtic brides and inter-married. As for Viking DNA, eastern

---

Did You Know?

Results may become more accurate in the future but the study of historic genetic material and its comparison to people living today will never be an exact science. For example, one survey discovered that the American president, Thomas Jefferson, and 87 other modern males with the same surname have ancient Egyptian genes!

England sees about 6% of Norwegian and Swedish DNA, whereas in Scotland and Ireland it's up to 16% but there is a problem with this. Many of the later Viking invaders were of Danish ancestry – just like the Jutes and Angles – so with present day methods of analysis the Danes have DNA too similar to the Anglo-Saxons to tell them apart.

What became of the Roman cities, towns and villas?

As we've seen, the Anglo Saxons and Celts appear to have lived in parallel, often in separate villages but why not move into the bigger urban centres? In order to run their huge empire efficiently, the Romans had an infrastructure of cities and towns from which their civil service could operate, collecting taxes and exercising the rule of law. Every important urban centre was connected to a network of roads which, ultimately – as the saying goes – all led to Rome. Major building projects were undertaken: bridges, aqueducts, forts, bath complexes, amphitheatres, market places [fora], municipal centres and fine country houses or villas, and many of these were built in stone. With ready-made urban buildings, it seems strange to us that once the Romans abandoned this outpost of civilisation, the cities and towns were mostly left to fall into ruin[1]. Why did the Anglo-Saxons prefer to live in wooden structures they erected themselves, rather than have stone walls and a tiled roof to keep out the weather?

10

In the past, historians have said that the Anglo-Saxons believed only a race of giants could have built so much in stone and, out of superstition, feared to live in such places. But they were a practical people and I think the reasons are more prosaic: cost and the lack of the appropriate skills.

Recently, a new way of looking at this is that at a local level, the humbler folk had seen little benefit from being part of the unwieldy Roman Empire, ruled from afar by those who only regarded Britannia as a resource. Heavy taxes, imposed foreign laws and the labour required for the export of home-grown cereals, textiles and minerals such as lead, copper, tin and silver was the poor man's experience of *Pax Romana*. Perhaps, like the UK in the referendum of 2016, when the people voted to leave the European Union, they were relieved to shrug off the tax burden and political machinations of distant governing elites and go their own way, ruling themselves. Whether the UK did the right thing is still up for debate but the Britons had little choice in AD 410 and maybe saw it as an opportunity to make the most of their new independence, rejecting almost everything Roman with the possible exceptions of Christianity and square buildings.

For the ordinary villager and his family, farming their plot, not much had changed in the way of life since before the Romans came and now, without this top-down influence, the simple day-to-running of local affairs without the bureaucrats, came to the fore, reasserting itself. No wonder we see similarities to the way Celtic society was organised four hundred years before. This wasn't a case of reverting to the old ways because those ways had never been discarded at local level, only submerged in Roman red tape.

By the time the Anglo-Saxons were here in significant numbers, half a century had passed since the Romans departed: five decades at least for their stone buildings to have fallen into disrepair, if not into ruin. The newcomers were brilliant at metal-working, boat building and seamanship, textile production and farming but working with stone was not one of their traditional skills. Carpentry and joinery were. Since they lacked the knowledge and tools to repair or rebuild

Lullingstone Roman Villa remains, Kent. Such buildings would be impossible to repair without the right skills and know-how.

a stone town house or country villa, it was quicker and easier to begin afresh and construct a new timber house. Besides, they might make use of the good Roman roads and stone bridges but had no need of baths, amphitheatres and large market places. If they had wanted to learn masonry techniques, it would have required buying in those skills from the Continent: an expensive and unnecessary luxury for a fledgling economy which had little or no remaining coinage.

We do know from archaeology that some country villas remained inhabited for years, often divided up between more than one family with rooms given over to workshops, cattle byres and grain stores while the estate, or parts of it, was still farmed.

But once the walls began to crumble and the roof leaked, they were left to fall down as the people moved out into new timber dwellings that they had the skills and materials to maintain in good order. As with so many of the events of this period, almost nothing was recorded in writing and these first 'English' people really did live in the 'dark ages', although archaeology is revealing more and more of their secrets every year, else they would be lost to us – almost.

Religion

When the Romans first occupied Britannia, both they and the Celts worshipped pagan gods. The Romans had Jupiter, the greatest god and his consort, Juno; Mars, the god of war; Mercury, the swift-footed messenger and god of merchants and markets, among other things. Venus was the goddess of love but there were a host of others: Apollo, Vulcan, Diana, Neptune and many more. The Celts had a more earthly group of deities, worshipping trees, springs and natural phenomena, possibly with an Earth Mother goddess over all. The Romans were content to combine their own deities with the local ones. For example, the town of Bath was a popular health spa frequented by the Romans but the natural hot springs there were worshipped by the Celts as a gift of their goddess Sulis. The Romans called the town Aqua Sulis, recognising the Celtic belief rather than obliterating it. The one aspect of Celtic religion the Romans eradicated was the Druids. This was most probably because the Druids held great power in Celtic society and were a danger to Roman dominance, rather than a religious threat.

But in the fourth century, Roman religious toleration of other cultures' pagan beliefs ceased when the Emperor Constantine announced that the entire empire had converted to Christianity, a religion which didn't allow for belief in any other deity but the one Almighty God. Quite to what extent everyone throughout the empire obeyed this imperial edict we don't know. There may have been localised worship of favourite pagan gods which quietly continued but, officially, the whole Roman Empire was now Christian. But around the fringes, where the Romans had never conquered or their influence was tenuous, pagan tribes, like the Angles, Saxons, Jutes and Scandinavian peoples still worshipped their own gods as they wished.

When the Roman legions withdrew in AD 410, did the Britons revert to their old pagan ways? Some may have done so but when Ambrosius Aurelianus raised men to fight the Saxons, his was a

Christian army intent on defeating the pagan invaders. Perhaps that is why the legendary King Arthur remained a popular hero for centuries even among the Saxons' descendents because, first and foremost, he was a Christian fighting against paganism and, in the seventh century, the Saxons, the Angles and other incomers were themselves converting to Christianity.

So let's take a brief glance at the religion of the Saxons when first they came to this country and, eventually, supplanted Roman Christianity for two centuries. Unfortunately, because theirs was not a literate society until after their conversion, we don't know very much about how they worshipped, whether they had religious leaders serving as priests and if acts of worship were held regularly and took a specific form. Bishop Sidonius wrote about what he termed 'Saxon pirates' saying 'it's their custom [after a raid] thus homeward bound, to abandon every tenth captive to a watery end. These men are bound by vows which have to be paid in victims; they conceive it as a religious act to perpetrate this horrible slaughter.'

Was this true and was it an aspect of the Saxon religion? We only have the bishop's word for it and he could have been simply passing on an exaggerated rumour or describing a one-off event which occurred in tragic circumstances, such as an overcrowded ship in danger of capsize when sacrificing a few saved the many. The trouble is that we only have the Christians' side of the story. But we do know that the Germanic tribes had a pantheon of gods though far fewer than that of the Romans in earlier times.

Woden was their chief or king of the gods, as well as being the god of wisdom. [The Norse religion called him Odin.] Woden's consort was the goddess of fertility, marriage and childbirth, Frig. [Freyr in Norse]. Tiw was the god of war [Tyr in Norse] and Thunor [Thor] was the god of thunder. Those were the main deities but there are others who have a mention here and there: Bede refers to Eostre, goddess of spring and rebirth from which we take our word 'Easter' – strange that the most important event of the Christian calendar is known in English by a pagan name. Eorthe, the Mother of Earth, crops up in a healing charm. Wyrd maybe the god who determines fate and Bede also writes of the goddess Hretha but doesn't tell us her context. Unusually, the sun is represented by the goddess, Sidgel, and the moon by her brother, Mone, rather than the sun being the dominant male and the moon the more retiring female deity. The Saxons also had a patron god, Seaxneat. There may well be other deities lost to history, their stories unknown now.

One aspect of the culture of the pagan speakers of Old English will never be forgotten, literally, in our everyday lives. Sunday is the day of the Sun; Monday that of the Moon. Tuesday is Tiw's day; Wednesday is Woden's day; Thursday is Thunor's or Thor's day and Friday is Frig's day. All named for the Germanic pagan gods. Compare this to French where Lundi is Luna's day [the Roman Moon goddess], Mardi is Mars' day; Mercredi is Mercury's day; Jeudi is Jupiter's day and Vendredi is Venus's day – all Roman gods. In English, who knows why, Saturday is still the Roman god, Saturn's day. Did the Anglo-Saxons not have a name for the best day of the week? They hadn't run out of gods, I'm sure.

But one thing we do know about Anglo-Saxon paganism was that it involved a strong belief in an afterlife and the dead were sent on their way with feasting and ceremony and all that they would need to boast of their status, keep them comfortable and ready to carry on as before in the hereafter. Historians are deeply grateful for this aspect of their religion because so much of our knowledge of the day-to-day activities of the Anglo-Saxons has come about through the detailed study of their grave goods, from simple clay loom-weights to fabulous swords, a few wisps of textile to gem-encrusted shoulder clasps, fine wine goblets to huge cauldrons, musical instruments to children's toys. All such artefacts have a tale to tell, as we'll see in this book of handy hints on how to survive in Anglo-Saxon England.

Chapter 2

Social Structure

If you're travelling back in time to Anglo-Saxon England, where will you fit into society? Will you be a thegn or a churl? Hopefully, you won't be the lowest of the low: a theow or slave. At the top of the social heap is the king and this is a very hands-on monarch, not a mere figurehead. In the fifth, sixth and seventh centuries, kingship can be short and brutal.

How to be a king

The king only reigns so long as he is powerful and wealthy enough to continually reward his loyal followers as a renowned 'ring-giver' – in other words, he gives them regular gifts of gold or land. You can probably realise from this that peaceful times are not an option because the king must wage continuous war against his neighbours and be victorious in order to have a constant supply of treasure and new land to distribute to his supporters. A single defeat or sign of weakness can spell disaster for a pagan or early Christian king. He may swiftly be replaced by a more powerful neighbouring king or by one of his own followers who proves stronger and has accumulated enough wealth to reward others. It's a matter of survival, not sentiment and being a nice, kindly king is a recipe for disaster.

This is one reason why kings are often quite keen to adopt Christianity. Almighty God approves of kings and if the king has the support of the Christian Church, he has the job for life – in theory, anyway – and is more difficult to overthrow. However, life can be desperately short, if your followers are determined to have a new leader.

This new leader, if he isn't a victorious neighbour, may come from among the king's brothers, sons and nephews as the idea of a royal dynasty catches on. These male relatives are the athelings or princes. They serve as the king's military captains in the field and dine at the top table. They also advise the king as his 'Witan' or royal council and, when he dies, they choose the most suitable candidate to succeed him. This won't necessarily be the eldest son or even a son at all. The Anglo-Saxons select a new king on merit, the man most likely to prosper the kingdom and defend it from its enemies. The very last Anglo-Saxon king, Harold Godwineson, was the previous monarch's brother-in-law, not a blood relative, but was elected by the Witan as the best man to defend England.

How to be an ealderman

Below the king and the athelings are the ealdermen or noblemen. They are responsible for law and order in the kingdom and, as such a thing becomes increasingly important, the administration. Ealdermen are also required to call up the militia in time of war. Known as the *fyrd*, this army consists of any or all able-bodied men summoned from across the realm, as many as required to serve for forty days. Being an ealderman isn't a hereditary job but, like kingship, the successor is often chosen from a particular family group. Our modern word 'alderman' comes from ealderman and refers to those chosen to hold authority in the larger towns, especially in London. As then, the title isn't hereditary but another word similarly derived is 'earl' and earldoms do gradually become inherited titles. By the tenth century, athelings, earls, archbishops and bishops form the High Witan or inner royal council.

Model of an Anglo-Saxon nobleman, St Wystan, in St Wystan's Church, Repton, Derbyshire.

How to be a thegn

Below the earls are the thegns. You can be a king's thegn, serving and directly answerable to him, or a thegn of slightly lower status serving an earl, although, ultimately, everybody answers to the king. If you serve the king or the earl with deeds of valour and honour, you can expect him to reward you generously. The king may even make you an ealderman or, in later centuries, an earl. You are expected to go with the king wherever he travels to act as his bodyguard and serve him in his hall and, of course, he needs a sizable entourage to appear impressive. A thegn's other duties may require you to carry out managerial jobs, such as making sure lesser folk garrison and keep fortresses in good order and oversee maintenance work on highways and bridges, so the *fyrd* can swiftly march to wherever the enemy threatens. As a top thegn, you are entitled to have a lesser thegn serving you.

But beware: poor service, especially failure to turn up for the *fyrd*, can have serious consequences. Loss of lands and titles could be the least of them: death is a possible result if you let down the king. On a brighter note – maybe – if anyone murders or maims you, as a thegn your 'wergild' or 'man-gold' price is very high. Wergild is a sort of insurance payout, calculated according to your rank in society and the severity of your injuries. It's all set down in legal documents [see Chapter 4] but, if you're illegally slain, other than in war or by accident, your family will receive twelve hundred shillings or the equivalent from the miscreant or his family.

How to be a churl

If you aren't a thegn, and there are only about 2,000 at a time recorded in the documents of Wessex and Mercia combined, the next rung down the social ladder is to be a 'ceorl' or churl. This isn't as bad as it sounds, though I know to say someone is churlish is a bit insulting today, meaning they're ill-mannered and rude, but the word use has changed. Churls are the 'free folk' and the backbone of Anglo-Saxon society. They have a house and own land which they farm, although there are churls of differing degrees with better or lesser standards of housing and the area of land they have. Land measurement is by the 'hide'.

You can't take a tape measure to mark out a hide's worth of land because it varies according to the fertility of the soil. Instead, a hide is reckoned to be an area large enough to grow sufficient food crops to feed an average household, so a hide of good land will be smaller than a hide of poorer land but in either case it would be worth about £1. For purposes of tax payment and other official matters, 100 hides – meaning about 100 households – are reckoned to form 'a Hundred', overseen by an 'ealder', the shire or county then comprising numerous hundreds.

However, where I live in Kent, in the Hundred of Toltingtrough – a long thin strip lying north to south, inland from the River Thames – the hundreds are grouped into 'lathes'. Lathes are land units unique to Kent, originating in the sixth century when the Jutes settled here. By the eleventh century, at the time of the Doomsday Survey, Kent has seven lathes from west to east: Sutton, Aylesford (including the Hundred of Toltingtrough), Milton, Wye, Borough (including the Isle of Thanet), Lympne and Eastry (including Kent's capital, Canterbury). This knowledge may help you, if your time-travelling takes you to Kent, when the local thegn demands you pay your taxes – your 'hearth-penny' tax must be paid on Ascension Day each year – or, if you're 'fyrd-worthy', it's time for you to serve in the *fyrd*, according to his rota.

For this latter reason, churls have to know how to use weapons of war, spears, bows and arrows and, for close-quarter fighting, the lethal seaxes. A seaxe is longer than a knife but shorter than a sword and you'll need a round, wooden shield with a heavy, metal boss in the centre which you can use to punch your enemy whilst you try to stab him with your seaxe. Customise your shield with a paint job your friends can recognise in battle that will also scare your opponents. Swords are incredibly costly, so you won't have one of those unless you're an ealderman, an earl or an atheling. A sword is a masterpiece of the blade-smith's art and each is unique so deserves a name: two swords used by Beowulf in his saga are Hrunting 'The Thruster' and Naegling 'The Nailer'. If you can afford a sword, give it good name such as 'Blood-spiller' or 'Flesh-ripper'. In facing a determined enemy, every little helps.

As a churl, you're also 'moot-worthy', that is entitled, if not required, to attend the 'folk-moot', a sort of local council to deal with affairs of the hundred. Should you have the misfortune to be murdered, your wergild price will be as much as 200 silver shillings. That's only a fraction of that of a thegn's but not to be sneezed at even so. If any of your kinsmen or kinswomen or your slaves are murdered or maimed by an outsider, you can expect monetary compensation for your loss of their input and labours in the household. If neither the evil-doer nor their family can pay the debt, either he or a family member must come to work as your slave until the labour equivalent of the debt is paid off. It's a form of community service to compensate the victims. What a good idea! And much better than the blood feud which was the pagans' old method of exacting retribution.

So now you know what to expect as an Anglo-Saxon churl in general but there are grades of churlishness, as you might say. Top of the social ladder of churls are the 'geneats' who pay rent, plus one pig a year, to their overlord thegn. They must reap and mow his land and take his surplus crops to market for him, carry messages far and wide and escort the thegn's visitors as well as provide entertainment. Some of these duties suggest that a geneat must have a horse to ride to take the messages and a wagon of some kind to take goods to market.

The next grade down from the geneats are the 'kotsettlers' who have a 'cott' or cottage and a plot of land but pay no rent. Instead, they work for their overlords one day a week throughout the year and three days a week at harvest but can be ordered to work at any time, if need be, at such duties as guarding the coast against a threatening enemy. Though they don't pay rent, they still have to pay the hearth-penny tax.

The lowest grade of churls is the 'geburs' whose lives are controlled by their thegn overlord. They must work on his land for at least two days every week and three during the crop sowing season in February and March and at harvest time. At Martinmas on 11 November, they must pay the thegn 23 sesters of barley and two chickens and, at Easter, a lamb or 2 pence. It gets worse… throughout the winter, geburs take it in turns to guard the thegn's sheep fold from wolves, foxes and other predators during the night. Yes, wolves are still prowling around in Anglo-Saxon England, so take your spear if you're on watch.

During ploughing time, each gebur has to plough an acre of the lord's land each week and find time to plough his own few acres as well. He has to prepare and sow the lord's seed too but must plant his own land with his own seed supply – no 'borrowing' of his lordship's seed. Two geburs together must pay for the upkeep of one of his lordship's hunting hounds and give the local swineherd six loaves of bread for taking the pigs to the woods in autumn to fatten them up on acorns and beech-mast.

This sounds like a lot of hard work for little benefit to the poor gebur but there are perks. His overlord has to give him two oxen to pull the plough and the cart, a cow for milk, six sheep for wool and seven acres of crop-growing land as well as a plough, farming tools and kitchen equipment. However, when the gebur dies, his lord takes everything back again, so who knows what happens to his widow and family? So, I advise you not to be a gebur, if you can avoid it. On the other hand, you could be a 'theow', meaning a bondsman (or bondswoman) or a slave.

Being a slave

Slavery is perfectly legal and acceptable in Anglo-Saxon society but it's not so dreadful as you might imagine from our modern image of slaves. Theows have rights. They can own property and earn money in their free time – although there won't be much of that. If they manage to earn enough, they can buy their freedom or their owners may set them free to atone for their sins on their deathbed. Even if that doesn't happen, slaves must be properly provided for and are entitled to be given, per year, twelve pounds weight of good quality corn, meat equivalent to two sheep and a decent cow. Slave women receive less: eight pounds weight of corn, one sheep or three pence for winter supplies. During Lent, when meat is banned, a sester of beans must be given and, in summer, whey for cheese-making or one penny to buy it instead.

Every slave has the right to gather fire wood and to receive appropriate 'supplies' at Christmas and Easter. They must have an acre of land to plough and grow their own crops and be allowed to gather 'a handful of harvest' from the owner's fields as well as any other 'necessary rights' agreed to beforehand. It may not be your first choice but, because of these rights, in times of famine or following Viking raids, folk sometimes voluntarily sell themselves and their families into slavery in order to survive the worst with a chance of buying their freedom in better times. If trouble befalls you, this may be an option but let's hope you don't have to resort to such a desperate measure.

Townsfolk

Anglo-Saxon England is far more rural than Roman Britain had been with most Roman towns abandoned but because the site of those places had usually been chosen for a good reason, such as a river crossing, a safe harbour or an important crossroads, the newcomers tend to settle close by the old towns. London is a good example. Although there is little archaeological evidence of early Anglo-Saxons living in the decaying Roman buildings, they understand the advantages of London's situation on the north bank of the River Thames with the bridge crossing and river bank suitable for building wharves and landing places for boats. As far as we know, King Aelfred is the first person of note to build a great hall within the Roman walls and repair them, creating London as a 'burgh' in the later ninth century.

Before that, there is an Anglo-Saxon settlement to the west of the London, outside the walls, in the area that is now Trafalgar Square and

Covent Garden, dating from around AD 500. The town is known as Lundenwic: 'wic' means a trading place. Lundenwic extends inland from the Thames between the River Fleet and Thorney Island – now known as Westminster – as far as present-day Oxford Street which is a Roman road leading west. Another road winds down to the Thames with drainage ditches on either side and alleyways leading off. Wattle-and-daub houses line the road and there is metal-working, bone-working, pottery and woollen textile production going on.

By the eighth century, Lundenwic is a bustling place under Mercian rule and the population is probably over 5,000, though this is small compared to Roman Londinium which had around 60,000 people living within its walls. Surprisingly, we know of two men who live in Lundenwic, both of whom, in an idle moment or two, carved their names in runic letters on a couple of mutton bones. How amazed they'll be to learn that those bones and their names will be rediscovered 1,500 years later! Let's have a word with Tatberht and Oethilward, two literate fellows of Lundenwic in the Hundred of Ossulstone in the shire of Middlesex.

'Good afternoon to you, Tatberht and Oethilward. I hope you are both well.'

'Who are you? Do we know you? How do you know our names?'

'I watched you scratching your names on those meat bones. Did you enjoy your dinner?'

'We did but if you're hoping to share it, you're too late. The roasted mutton is all gone.'

'Pity. But tell me about life here in Lundenwic. What do you do for a living?'

'Bit of this and that. Oethilward here's a blacksmith, aren't you, Oethy? Tell him about that fine sword you're making for Ealderman Edgar.'

'Mm, well, it's taking a long time… fine craftsmanship can't be rushed but it's going to be the best I've ever made, so far. Ealderman

Edgar deserves it: he's a good lord to us, isn't he, Tatberht? Promised me an extra three acres of good pasture and a yoke of oxen for it, when it's made.'

'Reckon it'll be worth more than that, Oethy. I think his payment is a bit mean, seeing all the work you've done, the hours spent heating, hammering and quenching, over and over. And does he expect you to garnish the hilt as well?'

'Course not. The goldsmith will do that. I'm only making the blade. Tell this fellow about the new weaving house you're building for the womenfolk, Tat. That'll impress him, whoever he is.'

'It's going to be the biggest weaving house in Middlesex; something Lundenwic can be proud of. Our women weave the finest woollen cloth in all Mercia, so it seems only right that they have the best house to set up their looms with wide shutters to let the light in to see their work. Feel this. See? My tunic's made of their good cloth: warm in winter and cool in summer. I've heard tell King Offa himself wears Lundenwic cloth. My wife Eahlswith is the best weaver and keeps the other womenfolk to their tasks. She orders all things in Lundenwic [laughs] even though Ealderman Edgar thinks he's in charge.'

'Tatberht's right. Women organise us. Always have done; probably always will. The ealderman has invited everyone to the mead-hall tonight for hall-joys. Are you coming?'

'Hall-joys? What are they? I'm new here, you see.'

'And ignorant. Not like us who can read and write. Hall-joys are entertainments: music, riddle-making, story-telling. Me and Oethy are scops, story-tellers. Have you heard the one about the hero Beowulf and the monster, Grendel?'

'Not now, Tat. Save your story for the mead-hall. You have a weaving house to build and I've got a sword to forge. Come on. Fare you well, stranger, until tonight. [aside] Talks funny, doesn't he, Tat? I could hardly make out a word he said. Where do you reckon he's from?'

'Wessex, maybe? Or down Kent way. They speak oddly there, so I've heard. Jutish talk, probably. If he comes to the hall-joys later, we can ask him, if you're that bothered?'

'I'm not; not really.'

What are Anglo-Saxon houses like?

The seafaring Anglo-Saxons know all about shipbuilding and are brilliant carpenters or 'treewrights' as they call them. Fashioning squared timbers, setting masts into keels and constructing planked, watertight hulls are skills that are just as useful in building houses here in England, where timber is plentiful. For example, to the north of Lundenwic is a vast expanse of ancient woodland known as Waltham Forest (parts of which remain in the twenty-first century as Epping Forest).

Archaeological pollen profiles show the forest at this time is dominated by lime trees – known as 'linden' – but the Anglo-Saxons cut down so many of them that they change the main tree species, permanently, to beech and oak with birch and hornbeam[1]. Perhaps the local folk cut down the lime trees specifically because the wood is marvellous for the detailed carvings with which the Anglo-Saxons love to decorate door jambs, lintels and furniture. It never gets woodworm and its inner bark can be used as string or for weaving mats and baskets. Lime makes good charcoal, too, and we know that Oethilward and his neighbours were using this for smelting iron.

However, they may be purposefully planting the new dominant species of oak and beech because these have their own uses. Oak wood is best for building mead-halls, houses and ships. Beech wood is ideal for making tool handles as it doesn't splinter. It's also used as fuel and for smoking fish to preserve it. Oaks produce acorns and beeches produce 'mast' or nuts, both vital for fattening the pigs in autumn.

Timber is the main building material, even for churches and royal palaces and this is why they don't last. Often, the sites of Anglo-Saxon houses and halls are identified by archaeologists because the

> ### 📌 Top Tip
>
> Knowing which trees give the best timber for which purpose will be a useful skill when you go time-travelling, so check this out before you leave the twenty-first century.

holes in the earth, dug for the massive supporting posts, appear as blackened circles in the soil. This is because they build using the 'earth-fast' method without footings or foundations, sinking posts, supporting staves and even the wall-timbers themselves straight into the ground. When the wood rots, turning the in-fill of soil black, the Anglo-Saxon villager simply rebuilds. Inside, the house is sparsely furnished with a basic bed, bench and a couple of stools but the central open hearth with a cauldron over, suspended from the rafters, makes it cosy.

In the past, we assumed the Anglo-Saxons built their houses partially sunken in the ground with roofs constructed like up-turned boats but experimental archaeology has proved this wasn't the case and our ancestors didn't live in dark underground hovels. This discovery was made at West Stow, Suffolk, the site of an abandoned Anglo-Saxon village. When archaeologists first reconstructed a house, using Anglo-Saxon methods on the original footprint of a dwelling, it began to fill with water, so something wasn't right. Another house nearby had been destroyed by fire over a thousand years ago and the burned timbers fell inwards but remained intact. Those of the side walls were over 6 feet, so a man could stand upright inside the building. The floor appeared to have been dug out below ground level but it was realised that there were joists to support floorboards over this space, just like a modern house. This meant air could circulate to keep the house dry and warm and, if the local water table allowed, the area under the floor might be used for storage, entered through a trap door. What a relief for you as a time-traveller: you won't be living like a mole and you'll be able to stand upright on proper floorboards.

If you live somewhere like West Stow, there are likely to be two larger buildings. One will be the Anglo-Saxon version of the village hall-cum-pub – the mead-hall – where the community spends its evenings, dining and drinking together, telling stories, singing, exchanging news of the men's latest hunt or fishing trip and having the ealder or lord make known his or the king's orders. The other large building is the weaving-house and, if you are a woman, this is where you will spend much of the day, turning wool or flax into textiles, not only to clothe yourself, your family and fellow villagers but, if the cloth is of good quality, to sell elsewhere. We know weaving goes on in Lundenwic because Anglo-Saxon loom weights have been found on the site of the Royal Opera House in Covent Garden.

But the weaving-house isn't just the place where women work. It's where the domestic decisions are made because while the menfolk are out farming and hunting, and although the village ealder thinks he's in charge, it's the women clothworkers who manage the day-to-day running of affairs in the community. Here, the women are at the heart

The reconstructed Anglo-Saxon weaving-house at West Stow, Suffolk.

of village life and probably make most of the important decisions. Sitting at their upright looms, they discuss ways to stretch the corn store for flour until the next harvest, remedies for childhood ailments and, fingers crossed, the men will catch a hare or two to go in the stew pot. Other matters will involve travel, perhaps to sell their cloth at market or barter it for necessities the villagers can't produce for themselves.

Unless they have a blacksmith locally – and this is rare because there isn't enough work for him in one small community – they must go elsewhere to buy vital knives, farm tools and axes, to have repairs made to ploughshares and cooking pots or to purchase pins and brooches to hold their clothes together. The Anglo-Saxon wardrobe doesn't require much sewing and pins or brooches keep your tunic and cloak in place. Maybe the most life-changing decisions the women make are those about arranging marriages: daughters are usually sent away to wed; sons stay at home and their brides come to them. Although the Anglo-Saxons never heard of genetics, they know the dangers of too much in-breeding in a small community,

Mead-halls

As you've probably begun to realise, Anglo-Saxon life is organised very differently from ours in the twenty-first century. Your neighbours are likely to be your relatives, by marriage at least if you're a woman, and the villagers come together for meals and relaxation when the day's work is ended. This daily gathering means the mead-hall must be large enough to accommodate everyone for the evening meal. However, it is also used to give shelter to both people and their animals in times of trouble, with its stout doors barred against storms and blizzards and protected from human enemies by the menfolk armed with pitch forks and pruning hooks, if necessary. The hall has side aisles like a Christian church even when folk are pagan. These aisles must be wide enough for a pair of oxen, yoked side by side, to be able to turn around. If you imagine how much room two hefty beasts require for this manoeuvre whilst fixed together at the shoulder by a wooden bar, that gives you some idea of the size of a mead-hall. There are stalls for horses and cattle and pens for sheep, goats, pigs, chickens and other livestock.

One such hall is mentioned in the Anglo-Saxon saga *Beowulf* . The mead-hall in this case is grand enough to have a name: *Heorot* (Hall of the Stag) and the king – the ring-giver – lives here, surrounded by his warriors who sleep in the hall, and entertains visiting people of importance. The construction of the huge hall with it high roof is the task of the skilled tree-wrights or carpenters who carve and paint the supporting posts and beams, the lintels, door jambs and shutters. Their work is exquisite and brightly coloured, the paint makes the timbers last longer, protecting it from the weather, so serves a purpose as well as creating an impression of wealth.

However, the mead-hall at West Stow village isn't very large so here it seems that after enjoying supper together, cooked over the communal hearth, the families go home to bed in their own houses. The unmarried men remain, left to drink mead, share bawdy jokes, be rowdy and loud without disturbing sleeping children, until they too slumber on the benches in the hall.

At Wychurst [pro. Wik-herst], near Hythe in Kent, *Regia Anglorum,* a national re-enactment group, constructed an enormous mead-hall on an original Anglo-Saxon site, faithfully recreating the wide aisles, the finely carved woodwork and wall paintings, discovering the pitfalls of plastering and making oak shingles for the roof. None of these ancient crafts is as simple as first thought.

In October 2012, an Anglo-Saxon mead-hall, dated to between the seventh and ninth centuries, was discovered by archaeologists beneath the village green at Lyminge, also in east Kent. This hall could accommodate up to sixty people and some of the finds there show it was of high status. Gilded horse harness decorations, jewellery, glass beads and bone combs and a bronze manicure set were dropped by the drunken merry-makers as they fled when the hall burned down after the last feast.

If your village has a typical mead-hall, what is it like to live in? Either at one end or halfway along one side will be the entrance, wide

The reconstructed mead-hall at Wychurst, Kent.

enough to allow those oxen through but it's not known for certain if Anglo-Saxon halls are like Christian churches with the most important area at one end or whether the dais for the lord or ealder was to one side in the length of the hall. Whatever the case, the main entrance is probably opposite the dais. Its double doors of mighty oak planks pivot on iron or wooden pins sunk into holes at the top and bottom of the door frame with a hefty timber to slot in place to bar the entrance. Windows are few, small and high up with shutters to close out the weather. There is no such thing as window glass, I'm afraid, so the hall is draughty. The cooking fires are often outside because of the danger of fat spitting on hot embers and setting the hall afire. Clearly, this precaution wasn't sufficient to protect the mead-hall at Lyminge.

Between the bays for the animals in the side aisles, the full width of the hall, like the nave of a church, is the living space. Here, another fire burns for warmth and light in a central hearth positioned between the raised dais and the door, so his lordship doesn't get too cold, flanked by important guests, with the women seated at the sides. A final bay [the gap between two adjacent supporting posts], may be screened off as a private area for the headman and his family.

At each end of the hall is a triangular gap called a gablet, formed between the rafters and the roof. This is open to the outside to allow smoke to escape from the hearth in the centre of the building. There is no chimney or central smoke hole and even the hall of a king is smoky and gloomy. We know about gablets because of a story the Venerable Bede tells us – we met him in Chapter 1 – about a man's life being like the flight of a sparrow. One winter's night, a sparrow flies in through the gablet at one end of the king's hall, into the warmth and light, before flying out the other end, back into the darkness and cold beyond. Bede uses this image to represent life, in that we know nothing before our birth; neither do we know what happens after death. A man's life is just those few brief moments in between, whilst he is in the warmth and light, like the little bird.

Interior of the reconstructed mead-hall at Wychurst, Kent.

Chapter 3

Home and Family

If you're travelling back in time to Anglo-Saxon England, what will family life be like? We've discovered something about your place in society and the sort of houses you may live in but a most important question concerns food.

What would I eat and drink?

Forget potatoes, cauliflowers, Brussels sprouts – you may be pleased about that – oranges, lemons and tomatoes. The Anglo-Saxons only have home-grown or wild vegetables and fruit in season so there isn't a lot of choice. Towards the end of the period, trade networks have expanded and grapes and figs are luxury imports but only for the wealthy. But there are carrots – small and dark red, parsnips – small and whitish, and tough wild cabbage which is just leaves and no heart. Onions, leeks, peas and beans are cultivated crops, the last two often dried to keep throughout the year. Wild garlic, sweet cecily – aniseed tasting, wild thyme, wild parsley, summer savoury, dill and water cress are all free, if they grow locally, as are burdock roots and dandelion leaves. Blackberries, sloes, hazelnuts and crab apples are also free from the wild but the apples are incredibly sour and a good deal of honey – there is no sugar – is needed to make them remotely palatable.

The Anglo-Saxons also cultivate wheat and barley with oats and rye being grown on poorer soils. Wheat is used for bread-making; barley for brewing ale. Oats make pottage for everyone. This is a sort of savoury porridge into which any vegetables, meat or fish scraps can be added. Dried peas can also be used to make a pottage and in

---

ἳ Top Tip

Whatever cereal is grown, watch out for the wild corn-cockle which often grows amongst the crop as its seeds are poisonous. The seeds of other plants which grow in cereal fields – cornflowers, corn marigolds and poppies – are safe enough in small amounts.

---

the twenty-first century we call this pease pudding and it comes in tins – delicious. If the soil isn't good enough to grow wheat, rye is an alternative, making dark bread.

Bread and pottage

Since bread and pottage are the staples of everyone's diet, whether king or slave, let's ask Ardith, the local baxter [a female baker], about how she makes bread for the village:

'Good day to you, Ardith. I see you're very busy but could you tell us how you make bread, please?'

'Well, every household needs bread, don't they? How come you don't know about it?'

'I've only just arrived in the village.'

'But every village must have a baker or baxter, surely? Oh, well, if you're so dim-witted, I'll explain. Firstly, you need grain. Here, we prefer wheaten bread and last year was a good harvest so we have plenty. In bad years, I might have to use rye or a mixture of grains, making darker bread which isn't so popular. If the gods curse us with famine, I may need to add acorns, beech mast or hazel nuts to stretch what little grain we have. But Freya has smiled on our harvest, so I'm using wheat.'

'What do you do with it?'

'Patience. I'm coming to that. Secondly, the grain has to be ground into flour. I spend hours kneeling at my rotary quern stone, grinding away. You do know what a quern is?'

'That thing? It's two stones, one on top of the other, with a hole in the top and is that a handle?'

'That's called the rynd and I can adjust it to grind different sized grains. The grain goes into the hole and what falls out between the two stones onto the cloth is gathered up and put back in again, over and over, until the flour is ground. I could take the grain to the water-mill…'

'Or the windmill?'

'Windmill? No such thing, you dunderhead. As I was saying… getting Osbert the miller to grind it for me would be quicker and less work but the price he charges! Do you know he keeps half a sack of flour for himself out of every four sacks-worth he grinds? I can't afford that so I make my own. That means I know it's good flour, no chalk dust added to it. I've seen Osbert do that, the wretch.'

'So your customers can trust you.'

'Of course. My reputation is unblemished. Now where was I? Oh, aye, thirdly… I put the flour into that trug or kneading trough and add water, mixing it by hand and adding a piece of dough from a previous batch to leven it.'

'Leven it? What does that mean?'

'It makes the bread rise but before that, I have to knead it, work it so the dough becomes stretchy. Then I cover it with a wet cloth and leave it beside my clay oven where it's warm, until the dough is twice the size. It's a mystery how that happens but it does. Then I shape the dough into loaves ready for the oven which I've heated by burning brushwood and shavings from the carpenter's inside it. Then I rake them out, put the loaves in and seal the wooden door with leftover dough.'

'Why do you do that?'

'What a dimwit. When the dough around the door dries and crumbles, the loaves are baked. Don't you know anything? Now get you gone for my next batch is done.'

A quern stone being used at Sandwich, Kent, by a member of *Regia Anglorum.*

The dough from an earlier batch of bread-making is added because it contains quite a lot of yeast – the levan – more than comes from yeast spores which occur naturally on the grain or in the air. The residue from ale-brewing also works. Keeping old dough for this purpose is the origin of sour-dough bread.

The Anglo-Saxons believe certain plants aren't just good to eat, they're magical. Also, three is a magic number and nine is even more powerful, being three times three. Therefore, they have a special Nine-Herbs Charm, guaranteed to cure every problem. Since we know the Anglo-Saxons enjoy eggs, here is a re-invented 'nine herb omelette':

> Whisk together two eggs with a dash of sea salt. If you're wealthy enough to afford it, you can add black pepper but this is a real luxury. Melt oil – though lard is more authentic – in a frying pan, add the eggs and cook gently until not quite set. Now add a pinch of each of the ground herbs – mugwort, plantain leaves, betony, chamomile, nettle, crab apple leaves, chervil and fennel. [Yes, I know that's only eight herbs but…]. Add some grated hard goats cheese. Fold the omelette and serve straight from the pan with fresh bittercress [the ninth herb] which tastes like rocket. There are some interesting flavours here so enjoy![1]

What is there to drink?

In your village, you may be lucky enough to have pear, cherry and plum trees but the pears will be hard. Even so, like crab apples which can be used to make cider, pears can be fermented into perry, both being sweetened with honey. Or honey itself can make alcoholic mead which often has herbal flavouring added. Meadowsweet is a popular flavour [meadwort in Old English] and perhaps not only for the taste because the plant contains a form of aspirin so will cure your hangover before it starts, if you drink too much mead. Ale is brewed from barley but it may have been flavoured with bitter hops so, technically, that makes it beer.

Evidence for hops comes from an archaeological find made in the Thames estuary off the town of Graveney [pro. Grainy] in Kent. A tenth-century inshore trading vessel, known as the Graveney Boat, was discovered sunken in the mud with wild hops among its cargo[2]. Since hops have no other use but to flavour and help preserve beer, we can assume that the Anglo-Saxons drink beer, though hops will fall out of fashion at some point, as folk prefer their ale to taste sweeter. Hops are re-introduced from the Netherlands in the late fifteenth century but not to universal appreciation. Wine is imported as a drink for the wealthy but homemade flower, fruit and herb wines, juices, cordials and tisanes can be made in season, so I'm sure you will find a drink to your taste.

Meat for dinner

So far, you might think the Anglo-Saxons are vegetarians but, given the opportunity, meat and fish are definitely on the menu. In fact, chemical analysis of early Anglo-Saxon skeletons shows that all levels of society, from slave to lord, ate meat frequently. Free meat can be caught by netting small wild birds or shooting various larger species – if you're good with a bow and arrow, a catapult or a sling shot – such as herons, cranes, bitterns, curlews, snipe and wild geese. Deer, wild boars and hares are hunted for food with dogs. So are wolves, foxes, otters and badgers but these last four aren't for eating but considered to be vermin because they prey on livestock or fish. Why badgers are thought to be a problem since they don't eat anything of value to man isn't clear and bovine/badger tuberculosis is unknown.

Domesticated livestock provides much of the meat you'll eat: cow, sheep and pig meat mainly but don't call it beef, mutton and pork as nobody will know what you mean. These are French words –

Did You Know?

On the subjects of diseases, measles is a virus which evolved from a cattle pathogen as recently in human history as the eleventh or twelfth century, so the Anglo-Saxons don't suffer from it. King Aelfred's people can't catch measles although there are plenty of other ailments to afflict them.[3]

boeuf, mouton, porc – used by the Norman lords after 1066 to name the meat on their plates but since their Anglo-Saxon serfs tend the animals, the live beasts are still referred to as cows, sheep and pigs.

Every animal has other uses besides providing meat. Sheep give milk and wool and the animals are kept until they're quite elderly, being shorn year after year, so when eventually they end up as meat, it's tough and has to be boiled to make it tender. Lamb can be an Easter Sunday celebration dinner but, otherwise, killing lambs to eat is a waste when you could have valuable wool off its back every summer. Cows and goats not only provide milk but horn which is made into drinking cups, book covers, lantern and window 'glass' and toggles for clothing. Their hides and those of pigs, too, can be turned into leather or even parchment for writing. Animal bone is useful for anything from tool and knife handles to jewellery, pins and sewing needles and sinew can be turned into bowstrings or used as strong thread for sewing ships' sails together. Nothing is wasted by the Anglo-Saxons and, who knows, maybe you'll be able to return to the twenty-first century with new ideas on a greener ecological society.

Early in the Anglo-Saxon period, pigs are the most popular meat. A sow produces a dozen or more piglets in one farrow – a litter of baby pigs – they eat anything, fatten fast and can look after themselves, so, pigs aren't too much trouble to rear. Their meat can be salted or smoked and hung in the *spic-hus*, the 'bacon and lard house' – the latter giving us the word 'larder'. However, later in the period, fewer pigs seem to be eaten – we don't know why – and more cows and sheep are consumed. Cows rather than bulls are allowed to grow to maturity because milk, butter and cheese are important. Bull calves are either slaughtered young or castrated to become the stronger and more docile oxen to pull the plough or wagon. Only a few bulls are kept for breeding purposes as cows must mate every year to keep up milk production and produce calves.

Sheep and goats are numerous but smaller than twenty-first century breeds – as are cows and pigs. Sheep can find grazing in places inaccessible to cows and some may even eat seaweed washed up along the shore. The ewes can be milked but it's time-consuming because it takes maybe ten sheep to produce as much milk as a single cow but ewes' milk makes good cheese. Animal fat is rendered down for cooking purposes and also to make tallow candles. These are far cheaper than beeswax candles which are usually reserved for church use or in noble households. Tallow burns with a smoky, yellow light and smells horrible, so you can see why the rich prefer beeswax.

Chickens provide eggs as well as meat for the pot, as do geese but the laying season is shorter than with modern breeds, mainly in spring and summer. Oddly, ducks don't seem to be popular at all and no one is sure why. Perhaps you can ask the locals. Because birds have hollow bones, those of chickens are ideal for making musical pipes and whistles.

Did You Know?

In the days before refrigeration was possible, milk quickly went sour. Butter and cheese have salt added which makes them last longer than milk. Hard cheese, made with the milk left behind after churning butter, keeps for years but needs soaking and hammering to soften it before it's edible. There is even a case of such a cheese being bequeathed in a will.

Fish on the menu

From archaeological digs, especially in latrine pits and middens – rubbish dumps – we know what kinds of fish were eaten because of the bones found. But written evidence comes from a colloquy composed by a teacher named Aelfric to help his students with their reading. The colloquy is in the form of a dialogue in which the 'Master' asks a 'Fisherman' about his work and the fish he catches. Fishing in the river using nets or baited hooks on lines, the fisherman lists pike, roach, perch, salmon, trout, lampreys and even minnows. Eels are caught in funnel-shaped baskets of woven willow. Sea fish are caught in surface nets or with hooked lines and include herrings, flat fish of various kinds, cod and whiting. Inshore, shellfish are collected and are big on the Anglo-Saxon menu so I hope you like oysters, cockles, mussels, whelks, crabs and lobsters. Note: oysters and lobsters aren't reserved for the top end of the market as they are in the twenty-first century: poor folk eat them too.

To preserve fish when it's plentiful, it can be salted, smoked, pickled or dried to keep for leaner times. An archaeological dig in Gravesend, Kent, in 2004, unearthed seven fire pits, dating to c.AD 485-510 and 500-530. Being close to the River Thames and with fish bones all around, these are thought to have been fish smoking pits.

One mystery you may be able to solve concerns rabbits. It used to be 'common knowledge' that the Normans introduced rabbits to this country and yet rabbit bones have been found in Anglo-Saxon archaeological

Did You Know?

Whales, dolphins, porpoises, seals, beavers and even barnacle geese and puffins are reckoned to be 'fish' in medieval times so, once Christianity is established and Lent becomes a no-meat, fish-only period of forty days, you can still eat these mammals and birds and be approved by the Church.

sites. Certainly, the animal isn't mentioned by name in any writings but they seem to be on the menu. Can it be that they are thought of as a type of hare because hares are mentioned numerous times in texts?

How would I cook my food?

Cooking is generally a job for women. When an Anglo-Saxon army is on campaign, there are wives, sisters, daughters and assorted camp followers to prepare meals which are usually of the one-pot kind: stews and pottages, the thicker and more filling the better, boiled in a cauldron over a fire. Any game caught on the march can be wrapped in wet leaves or clay and cooked in the embers. Apparently, hedgehogs can be cooked in this way, wrapped in damp clay which is then broken open like an egg shell and comes away, removing all the prickles!

Away from home, bread will be flatbread rather than leven bread and can be baked on a griddle over the fire or on a hot stone. This is also an alternative at home, if there's no time to let the bread rise.

♪ Top Tip

Don't try this in the twenty-first century as hedgehogs are a protected species in the UK.

If you're poor, meat isn't going to be on the menu very often unless you net wild birds, a chicken dies of old age or a sheep meets with an accident. Otherwise, your best chance of a meaty meal will be if your lord invites you to his table and this is likely to be a men-only affair, unless it's a special celebration such as a wedding. How often you eat meat is a matter of status. Bacon is suitable for cooking on a hanging griddle over the fire but frying pans also exist and, of course, frying saves the precious fat which shouldn't be wasted – you can use it to help waterproof your boots or even your cloak, if you don't mind smelling of rancid pig when the fat goes off.

Cooking meat on a griddle.

In the summer and early autumn, fresh vegetables and meat are at their most plentiful but in winter and spring you'll probably have to make do with dried or pickled veg, salted, pickled, smoked or dried meat and fish. When an animal is slaughtered, as I've said, nothing is wasted. The blood is collected, stirred as it cools to prevent clotting, then salt, flour and herb flavouring are added. The mixture can then be stuffed into the thoroughly washed intestines of the animal to make black pudding – a blood sausage – or shaped into little patties and fried like burgers.

There is evidence of a most unusual – and risky – cooking method found in two Anglo-Saxon manuscripts which involves prepping diced pork and chicken which are put into a small earthenware pot with salt and spices and the lid sealed with moist clay. This pot is then put inside a slightly larger earthenware pot filled with water. Now comes

Did You Know?

There's a tradition of killing surplus animals at the beginning of winter if there isn't enough hay and fodder to last them through to the spring. Later, the 11 November, St Martin's feast day, becomes the customary date for this event and it's known as the Martinmas Slaughter.

the risky part. Quicklime, which is VERY caustic, is added to the water, setting off a violent chemical reaction which creates a lot of heat. 'Let stand for the time it takes to walk between five and seven leagues' and your food will be cooked, so the recipe says[4]. I advise you to leave this to an expert cook especially as it requires a lot of walking: a league being about 3.5 miles or 5.5 kilometres by which time you will definitely have earned your dinner.

The best joints of meat or poultry can be spit-roasted. A wild boar or ox on a spit, roasting over a large hearth, is what we imagine as the centre piece of an Anglo-Saxon feast but, on a smaller scale, cubes of meat or small birds can be cooked on skewers, like kebabs. Along with plenty of drink – most probably alcoholic – this is at the heart of a feast but bread, pottage and vegetables will all appear. There may even be a sweet dessert.

For a sweet dessert, you need a sweetener, obviously. Sugar isn't known here until the Crusaders discover it in the Middle East in the eleventh century and imported sugar remains an expensive luxury until the seventeenth century. So how do you sweeten those sour fruits? The answer is honey. The local beekeeper is a vital member of every community. In spring, when your fruit tree is in blossom, you pay him/her or barter with him to bring his hives – often woven from reeds and known as 'skeps' – to your garden so the bees can pollinate the flowers and you'll get a good crop of fruit in the autumn. The bees will use the nectar gathered from flowers throughout the summer to make honey in the hives. The beekeeper then profits a second time from selling the honey.

Figures suggest that a healthy hive can produce 100lbs of honey a year and that a household of six people will need about ½lb of honey every day[5]. Apart from using honey to make mead or to sweeten sharp fruits or maybe simply spreading it on bread, there is evidence that the Anglo-Saxons may have enjoyed a dessert, at least on special occasions. Sadly, in the twenty-first century, we lack a proper recipe book from this period. Maybe cooking is so simple that methods are memorised and passed on from mother to daughter. As we know, some people are literate but ink and parchment are costly, used for legal and religious documents and books, and not to be wasted on something so trivial as noting down how to make a cheesecake. Perhaps when you return, you can tell us some of the best recipes you've learned. It's thought that honeyed almond cakes, sweet spiced bread and – yes – a kind of cheesecake may well have been served at a feast. And this brings us to the subject of presenting and serving the meal.

How would I serve a meal?

Like cooking, serving drinks at table is down to the women and even a queen isn't exempt from pouring the mead for an important guest. It's thought that some of the most splendid cauldrons discovered as grave goods, like the one found at Sutton Hoo, are not for boiling mutton stew over the fire. They're far too grand and show no signs of soot blackening or being heated over flames. Instead, these elaborate great vessels are probably for serving drinks. Either the serving woman dips a jug into the cauldron and then fills the cups, or each drinker can simply dip their beaker directly into the ale, probably in a bucket, if this isn't a noble meal.

Food is eaten from wooden boards or clay bowls, if it's pottage or stew. Spoons are provided but don't forget to bring your own knife. It's not rude to bring your own cup as well, if you have one you prefer or want to show off! Cups of bronze, silver or glass make quite an

The Sutton Hoo hanging bowl or cauldron.

impression, if you're wealthy enough to have one. Drinking vessels don't have handles and may be bowl-shaped or beaker-shaped. Decorated ox-horns are an Anglo-Saxon's traditional drinking vessel but only for those very serious about their drink because you can't put them down, unless there are special stands invented to support them about which we don't know.

You're allowed to eat meat off your knife, if it's too hot for fingers. There are no forks as such but digs on Viking sites have uncovered 'food-sticks' of wood or bone. Are these used as kebab skewers or for spearing chunks of gravy-soaked bread or pieces of meat? Do Anglo-Saxons use them too?

Once the men are fed and happy, the women and children can eat at a separate table, followed by servants and slaves last of all, sharing bowls and cups and the left-overs. I know this sounds as though women get a poor deal but that's not entirely true. In Chapter 2, we heard how the women of the village run the day-to-day affairs of the community and Anglo-Saxon women do much better in the eyes of the law concerning marriage, divorce and when it comes to inheriting land and property.

BUCKET

This small bucket was used as a food or drink container. The body and base are made of beech wood held together by copper alloy hoops with a handle of leather.

Glassware and drinks bucket in Dartford Museum, Kent.

What is life like for a woman?

Maybe the village women have found you a husband, if you're of a suitable age. As a recent arrival in the village, any unmarried son can consider you a possible bride, unless you make it clear that you intend to become a nun, if Christianity has arrived. Even then, convincing an eager bridegroom that you're not interested may be difficult. The first thing he will want to know is your bride-price. This is the groom's payment to the bride's parents and family for the cost of raising her to womanhood and educating her in a wife's duties. So, as an incomer without a family to demand your bride-price, you're bound to be cheap and, therefore, popular as a would-be bride.

In an ancient book known as the *Textus Roffensis* kept at Rochester Cathedral in Kent – it literally means the 'Rochester book' and we'll hear more about this in Chapter 4 – there is a charter from the early tenth century regarding the matter of arranging a marriage[6]. Firstly, the groom has to promise that if the woman agrees to marry him – she does have a choice – he will treat her as both God's law and custom demand and pay the bride-price demanded by her family. His kinsmen are to ensure he does both these things. If she isn't keen (and it's worth playing hard-to-get), he may have to bribe her to accept him. For example, Godwine wished to wed Brihtric's daughter and gave her a pound weight of gold, if she would accept him, to be followed by his estate at Street and everything that went with it, 150 acres of land at Burmarsh, thirty oxen, twenty cows, ten horses and ten slaves, if the marriage should be 'agreeable to her'[7]. That's quite a bribe, isn't it?

Secondly, he has to say in advance what he will give the bride if she marries him. This will be a piece of land or property which will be hers to do with as she wishes. It's sometimes referred to as the 'morning gift' or *morgengifu*, bestowed on the morning after the wedding once the marriage has been consummated satisfactorily in bed. It's all about producing heirs so it's vital the couple are compatible. The groom also has to state which of his properties and estates will be hers, if she outlives him. Later on, this is known as the widow's dower. Usually, she gets half of his estate but, if they have a child together, she gets all of it with the idea that the child will eventually inherit everything. The groom's kinsmen are to guarantee this happens unless the widow remarries, in which case everything is up for discussion.

Once all this is agreed, the couple are officially betrothed. However, if the groom is from another place and wants to take his new wife to live there, his family must assure her overlord that they'll keep her safe. And if the lord demands compensation for her leaving his village – perhaps she's a brilliant weaver and he'll lose her income – then the groom's relatives must pay her lord a fee, if the bride can't afford it.

Finally, the contract gets to the actual wedding: that by law a priest must be present to join the couple 'in all prosperity' and bestow God's blessing upon them. Then, as an afterthought, is added that the bridal pair must check with their families on both sides to make sure they're not too closely related. You won't have to worry about this because the nearest kin you are likely to be to your bridegroom is if you are his twenty times plus great-granddaughter.

Once you are married, all the property is jointly owned between husband and wife. Both partners can make gifts and donations to religious foundations, lend money to royalty, etc. But supposing things turn sour in the marriage. Fortunately, Anglo-Saxon law allows

Did You Know?

Interestingly, after 1066 and until the eighteenth century, the law doesn't require a priest to be present for a marriage to be legal. Also, it may sound odd but the Anglo-Saxons thought of a female as a 'man' – as we use the term 'mankind' to refer to both – showing that males and females were equal but with different parts to play: *waeponmenn* = 'weapon-people'; *wifmenn* = 'weaving-people'.

🔖 Top Tip

If Granny has recently died, been buried with grave goods and you can't find the keys to the store cupboard or money box… oops! You know where to look.

---

divorce and it's so simple: according to the seventh- and early eighth-century laws of King Aethelberht of Kent, the wife has the right to walk out of the marriage if she isn't happy. If she takes the children with her, she's also entitled to take half the property.

Archaeology also shows how women are regarded in Anglo-Saxon society. Women's graves from the pre-Christian period contain goods to aid them in the afterlife, revealing their status. Some are buried with fabulous jewellery to show their wealth; others with girdle-hangers and/or the keys which hang from them. It seems that women have charge of the household keys. This idea is supported by a later law from the reign of King Cnut [r.1016-35] which states that a wife can't be accused of theft if her husband steals goods and hides the loot in their house unless the ill-gotten gains are discovered in one of three places, namely, in the *hordaern* or storeroom, the *cyste* or chest for valuables, or the *teag* or jewellery box. If stolen goods are found in any of these places, the wife is her husband's accomplice because, it is taken for granted, she holds the keys to them.

Gavelkind

You may not have heard this word before but you'll be familiar with the concept. Whereas the later Normans insist that the eldest son should inherit the titles and the estates of his father, except in exceptional circumstances, the Anglo-Saxons have gavelkind. Gavelkind means that all the children, both sons and daughters, share the inheritance equally. This sounds much fairer but can lead to difficulties.

Imagine an estate of medium size shared between four children who then go on to have offspring of their own. In just a few generations, a workable estate has become so divided into smaller plots that no one has enough land to turn a profit or even feed a family. That would be the logical outcome but it rarely comes to that. Amicable agreements between the siblings usually mean that one or other of them – not necessarily the eldest son – takes on the bulk of the estate, compensating the others with money, livestock or equipment. Or all four and their families continue to work the entire estate, sharing the profits equally. High mortality rates often reduce the number of those between who the profits have to be split but there are plenty of records which show that brothers, sisters, nephews, nieces and cousins happily get together to sort out how their inheritance is best divided to benefit them all.

Family and kinfolk are all important to the Anglo-Saxons. Without family, you are nothing, an outcast, so get yourself adopted or married as soon as possible. It's the best way to survive.

Of course, there must be occasions when gavelkind doesn't work out to please everyone involved, in which case we have to turn to the law which we'll look at in Chapter 5. But before the Anglo-Saxon laws can be first written down in the late seventh century, the people need to become literate. And literacy arrives here with the Christian missionaries, so let's see how the pagan Anglo-Saxons are converted to a new [to them] religion.

Did You Know?

After William the Conqueror invaded England in 1066, he didn't 'conquer' Kent but came to an agreement with the people there. Among the concessions William made was that the people could continue with gavelkind inheritance, if they didn't make trouble for him as he subdued and conquered the rest of England. Kent still uses the motto 'Invicta', meaning 'Unconquered' and gavelkind was never revoked as far as I know.

Chapter 4

Religion – Paganism versus Christianity

As I mentioned in the Chapter 1, when the Anglo-Saxons first arrive here they're pagans, worshipping the gods Woden, Thunor, Tiw and Frig but what we don't know is what form that worship takes. Are there special places devoted to a particular god? We know certain days of the week are named after a specific god, so is that day set aside to worship that deity?

Are there shrines, idols and temples where worship takes place and is there a class of priests to oversee or control what goes on? Does worship involve animal sacrifice? We have so many questions but as pagans the Anglo-Saxons don't write anything down so all this information is never recorded and mostly lost to history. Neither have archaeologists discovered the remains of any building that can be definitely identified as having had a religious purpose but some Christian writers suggest that the Anglo-Saxons did construct temples to their heathen gods and have carved idols, though none have ever been found for certain[1].

Here is an extract from a letter written by Pope Gregory to Mellitus who was, briefly, Bishop of London: 'The idol temples of that race [the English] should by no means be destroyed, but only the idols in

---

↓ Top Tip

The Anglo-Saxons never refer to their previous beliefs as 'pagan'. Once converted to Christianity, they use to word *haethen* when mentioning the old gods.

Woden, chief of the Anglo-Saxon gods.

them. Take holy water and sprinkle it in these shrines, build altars and place relics in them. For if the shrines are well built, it is essential that they should be changed from the worship of devils to the service of the true God. When the people see that their shrines are not destroyed they will be able to banish error from their hearts and be more ready to come to the places they are familiar with, but now recognising and worshipping the true God.'

This is a very clever ploy because it means the locals can still attend their place of religious worship as usual but they will now be revering the Christian God instead of the old deities – whether they approve the change or not.

Another story tells of a Northumbrian priest who converts to Christianity in AD 627, giving us an interesting insight into the way gods are worshipped. This is what Coifi has to say:

'Coifi, I understand you're the chief priest here at Goodmanham in the kingdom of Northumbria.'

'That was true.'

'Was?'

'Yes. Being a priest gave me no advantages, I realised. I wasn't allowed to carry arms even to defend myself. Neither was I permitted to ride a decent horse. My position didn't bring me wealth, privilege or even particular favour with King Edwin, though he did occasionally ask my advice.'

'What were your duties as a priest?'

'What does it matter now? I dedicated my whole life to the gods, serving them with food and drink, dusting their wooden statues and instructing the people how to keep in favour with them because they can be fickle and testy, if you upset them. And what did the gods do for me in return? I'll tell you: nothing. Nothing at all! They're not worth the trouble. A lord rewards his servant but not Woden, the miserable old so-and-so. No reward for poor Coifi, for all his time and effort.'

'So what did you do?'

'I listened to the missionary – an odd fellow, it's true – calls himself Paulinus. He's been telling Queen Aethelburga this stuff for ages but I never took much notice before but last week I'd had enough of Woden and his lot. It was my son's wedding day and I asked Thunor specially to give us good weather for the celebrations. What happened? It poured with rain all day. They couldn't be bothered to grant me that one small favour.'

'And you blame the gods for that?'

'Of course. Who else decides when it should rain or shine? Anyway, I thought it was worth giving Paulinus's god a chance to show what he could do. During the wedding, I'd dropped my favourite brooch somewhere in the mud so I asked this new god to find it for me. And next morning, there it was, glinting in the sunshine right outside my door. So, when Edwin asked my advice about converting to Christianity, I told him to go ahead.'

'And he agreed?'

'Well, I helped things along a bit by going to the temple and knocking Woden's statue off its shelf and all the others. Idols, Paulinus calls them, and idle they were whenever I asked a favour. Then I took a flaming spear and cast it into the building. With the whole place gone up in flames, we'll all have to worship the new god, won't we? Even you, you heathen.'

This story – without the bit about the wedding and the lost brooch – was recorded by Bede in the eighth century in his *Ecclesiastical History of the English People*.

Why are the English converting to Christianity?

This is a good question. The Anglo-Saxons have been worshipping Woden, Thunor and the other gods for centuries back in their previous homeland and here in their new country. On the whole, the gods must seem to serve them well, unless like Coifi they've suffered personal disappointment. Both Roman writers like Tacitus and the much later British monk Gildas, writing around the middle of the sixth century – his dates are uncertain – describe England as a land of plains and gentle hills, fertile soils, green pastures, clean springs and rivers full of fish. Crops and fruits grow in abundance and game and livestock grow fat. England sounds like a paradise, though Gildas goes on to mourn its 'ruination' by war between the Britons [his people] and the new arrivals but he is exaggerating. Conflict is localised and small scale. However, it's obvious that this land is well worth having and it seems the old gods were smiling when the Anglo-Saxons set up home here. So why abandon those gods for a new belief system which has yet to prove its value to you? I think the answer may lie in the subtle changes that are happening in society.

When the Anglo-Saxons first arrive they come as mercenary bands in the pay of the Romans to help support the reduced troop numbers and repel the Picts and Scots in the north. Recent research has shown that Hadrian's Wall was still garrisoned in the last years of Roman occupation although the legions had been mostly withdrawn to defend the empire's heartland at the end of the fourth century. Later, it was the Britons who paid the mercenaries with land and provisions to defend the southern shores from pirates and invaders, including other Angles, Saxons, Jutes, Swedes and Frisians.

The mercenaries realise this land is an ideal place to start a new life. Families and kinfolk arrive and set up home. This isn't organised colonisation; it's a free-for-all. Nobody is 'in charge'. Only gradually, as more people arrive, does any kind of hierarchy begin to develop. It may be as simple as one family grabbing a slice of land which proves especially fertile and easily defined and defended. That family becomes wealthier than the neighbours and begins to pay others to help work their land and defend it. The head of that family exerts his influence over a wider area; other little settlements look to him to defend them from hostile neighbours. He becomes the local chief and, if things go well, by the time his grandson is head of the family, he calls himself 'king'.

It seems there are dozens of little kingdoms to begin with, developing in the early decades of the sixth century. Some, like Wessex, Mercia,

Northumbria, East Anglia and Kent, go on to become more powerful, swallowing up lesser kingdoms, such as Hwicca and Lindsey – which are lost to history – and some whose names survive, like Middlesex, Essex and Sussex. Gildas, who describes his land in such glowing terms above, has nothing good to say about these men who 'call themselves kings'. They are 'tyrants', he says. 'They plunder and terrorise, have multiple wives and mistresses and reward robbers. They despise the harmless and humble but exalt to the stars their military comrades: bloody, proud and murderous men.' These kings are the 'Ring-givers' of the Anglo-Saxon tale of *Beowulf.* [see Chapter 8]

But why now? Suddenly, in c.536, this island isn't a paradise any longer: the weather turns cold and crops fail and this pattern is repeated in subsequent years. In the 1980s, modern science discovered that a volcano in Iceland erupted in 536, 540 and again in 547, shrouding the sun in a dust cloud across the northern hemisphere. A contemporary Irish monk records 'failure of bread' at the time and recent analysis has concluded that the period between 536 and 547 was the coldest decade in the last 2,000 years[2]. Then, spreading west from Constantinople, comes bubonic plague. By 544, it reaches Ireland. The population of Europe is devastated; social structure and trade networks collapse. Now is the time for strong leaders to step up and hold everything together and if plundering your neighbours' meagre supply of food is the only way for the kinship group to survive, then so be it. These are desperate and turbulent times and the most likely explanation for the rise of kings. [If you have a choice in the matter, I would advise you not to travel back to Anglo-Saxon England at this period.] One of the earliest named kings, though historical proof is lacking, is Aelle, King of the South Saxons [Sussex] who may have ruled around 550. Another is Caewlin of the West Saxons [Wessex] who ruled in the 570-80s before being pushed out in 592, having plundered many villages, if the *Anglo-Saxon Chronicle* has its facts straight.

Woden is regarded as chief of the gods but otherwise the Anglo-Saxons' religion is quite egalitarian. Everyone can worship the god who suits them or the occasion best. The Anglo-Saxons also revere the landscape, much as the Celts did before the Romans came, and that includes sites which were important to the Celts and to the builders of the Neolithic and Bronze Age. Anglo-Saxon settlements are sometimes founded on top of Iron Age hill forts which, obviously, are good defensive positions but Bronze Age burial mounds and barrows are also reused. At Lyminge in Kent, three successive mead-halls are built on what was once a burial mound a thousand years before but remained visible in the landscape[3]. The burial sites of previous peoples are not only respected but used for the same purpose by the Anglo-Saxons, adding a new chapter to millennia of continuity in their new land, giving them a heritage here and making them part of this ancient story with a sense of belonging. That's a marvellous idea, isn't it? And a great way, not only to survive, but to live, put down roots and thrive in your new home.

But this old religion has nothing much to say about society or the place of kings in it. In the Anglo-Saxons' old homelands, kings don't figure in the story to any great extent but now, being a king in this new place has meaning and significance though, as we saw in Chapter 2, kingship is perilous and often short-lived when the wealth runs out or there's a new big man in town. And the gods have let everyone down, doing nothing to help in these times of famine and pestilence. Neither do they seem to bolster the idea of kings in any significant way, so royal families – as we may now call them – could be looking for a new sort of deity who understands the meaning of kingship and will be more helpful when times are bad. Yet an alternative takes another fifty years to arrive in southern England although in some areas, it's already here, lying dormant, or on its way across the Irish Sea.

The Pope and the 'Angels'

Meanwhile, so the story goes, in Rome in AD 595, Pope Gregory I – later known as 'the Great' – is strolling around the forum or marketplace, on the lookout for a new slave or two. There's not much to choose between what's on offer. Most are of Mediterranean lineage with dark hair and eyes, olive skinned, or darker. But then the pope sees some striking slave boys who appear completely different with fair hair, blue eyes, well-built and tall. Such a novelty would look stunning, waiting upon him in the palace.

'What are they?' the pope asks the slave master. 'Angles,' comes the reply. 'Not Angles but Angels', Gregory is supposed to have insisted. He then asks where they've come from and, most importantly, whether or not they're Christian. When he hears that the Angles are pagan, he determines that won't be the situation for much longer, if he has his way.

The pope summons a few of his most trustworthy monks who, he thinks, might relish a chance to travel and are up for adventure. Augustine, the Prior of St Andrew's Abbey in Rome, is first choice. Gregory is keen to send these men as missionaries to convert the Angles and any other pagans they find on that green and foggy island across the sea from Gaul. But the monks are doubtful and try to talk their way out of it. The pope is determined. Augustine and his not-so-merry band of forty reluctant missionaries are told to pack their bags: they're going to the land of the Angles, like it or not. It's all arranged.

We don't know the details of these arrangements but Pope Gregory had exchanged letters with Bertha, a Frankish princess married to King Aethelberht of Kent, and written to her royal Frankish kinfolk on the European side of the Channel. The Franks are already Christians and agree to supply priests and interpreters to join the missionaries, so, when Augustine arrives in Kent, he and his fellows are probably expected. They make landfall on the Isle of Thanet, just as the legendary ancestors of King Aethelberht, Hengist and Horsa, had supposedly done almost two centuries before. The place is carefully chosen for a number of reasons, as is the Kingdom of Kent, for a first mission to convert the heathens.

As I said, Aethelberht is wed to Bertha and the king allows her to continue practising her religion and have Christian priests, so he must know something of what his wife's religion involves and it's not entirely unfamiliar to him. Besides, Kent has close trade and diplomatic ties with Christianised Frankia. Also, Aethelberht himself is the powerful *Bretwalda* or 'High King' in AD 597 with influence throughout England and contacts with all the 'lesser' kings of the day[4]. This means he could persuade other kingdoms to consider converting to this new religion, if the missionaries are successful in Kent. And probably an excellent reason for coming to Kent, as far as the missionaries are concerned, is that the sea voyage from the European mainland is the shortest.

According to Bede, who, admittedly, is writing 150 years after the event and isn't always reliable, the king agrees to meet Augustine and his monks on open ground, being suspicious of what these foreigners might intend. The monks hold up a great silver cross – likely to impress the king – and explain why they are here. They appear harmless enough and although he's not convinced himself, Aethelberht gives them permission to preach their religion to the people of Kent. Better still, he grants them the use of St Martin's Church for their services. This church is in his capital of Canterbury, already used as a place of worship for Bertha and her Frankish priests and, with a Roman chancel, it may have been a Christian church before Rome withdrew the legions.

Later that year, Aethelberht agrees to be baptised into the Christian religion, probably in Canterbury, and thousands of his subjects follow his lead in a mass christening on Christmas Day 597. Whatever, their [or your] personal beliefs, it's a good idea to convert if the king has done so. It's the safest option if you want to survive but we know that many folk hedge their bets, worshipping the new Christ and the old Woden, just to be sure. What probably persuades Aethelberht that Augustine's god is a good choice for a king to worship is his book: the Bible. The Old Testament is particularly appealing with two books dedicated to Kings, whether good, bad or indifferent, and numerous demonstrations of the wrath of God.

This new God can bring famine and pestilence – horrors of his grandfather's day – but can also save the favoured ones and spare them from such nightmares. The Anglo-Saxons certainly understand this

The Anglo-Saxon nave of St Martin's Church, Canterbury, Kent.

concept. But the Bible also stresses the specialness of kings, that they are 'chosen' by God and receive divine authority. Aethelberht must love the sound of that when the old gods have nothing to say on the subject. The Christian God definitely approves of kings, being one himself, and understands exactly how social hierarchy ought to work: kings should rule and the lower, poorer sort must behave, do as they're told and be grateful for it, doing nothing to try and change things because the Christian God has ordained it so. Aethelberht is astute and realises his fellow kings will probably like that message too.

Spreading the Word

Augustine has made a splendid beginning to his mission and things progress marvellously. The king gives him land in Canterbury to found an abbey and a cathedral – literally a bishop's seat, but nothing too grand at first. In 604, one of Augustine's fellow missionaries, Mellitus, is sent to London, an important trading post on the River Thames and then part of the Kingdom of the East Saxons. With Aethelberht's backing as *Bretwalda*, Mellitus finds it easy to convert King Saeberht who is the King of Kent's nephew, his mother Ricula being Aethelberht's sister who wed Sledd, King of Essex. Saeberht gives Mellitus a plot of land on which to build a church as a cathedral: St Paul's. This isn't really much of a gift because it's in the ruined Roman city of Londonium where nobody lives, the Anglo-Saxons preferring their own settlement of Lundenwic a little farther upstream, half way between Londinium and Thorney Island.

Thorney – 'the island of thorn bushes' – is surrounded on two sides by a split in the River Tyburn and on the third side by the Thames into which the Tyburn flows. This unpromising place of brambles and marsh becomes the site of Westminster Abbey, dedicated to St Peter and said to be founded by Saeberht and his wife as their future place of rest. Although this doesn't seem to happen, Saeberht's pagan sons having other ideas about the burial of their parents, this 'West Minster' and its London counterpart St Paul's or the 'East Minster', will become important to the spread of Christianity, the spiritual and physical welfare of the local communities.

From the beginning, St Paul's in London and Mellitus are intended for greatness. London is at the hub of the old Roman road network which is still serviceable for the most part, placing it more at the centre of things than Canterbury. Because of this key location, Pope Gregory plans that Mellitus should become Archbishop of London, head of the Christian Roman Church in England, with his headquarters in St Paul's but this is when things go badly wrong for the missionaries.

Mellitus is just getting his nice new church set up and thinking of all the brilliant things he can do as an archbishop when, in 616, King Saeberht dies. This is terribly inconvenient because around the same date, on 24 February, King Aethelberht dies too. Suddenly, the mission's two powerful patrons are gone. Aethelberht is buried in St Augustine's Abbey, founded by him in 598 in Canterbury, then known as Sts Peter's and Paul's until Augustine is canonised and it's rededicated in his name. In Kent, there is a temporary set-back from a religious point of view because the king's son, Eadbald, who succeeds him, isn't so keen on Christianity and Justus, the Bishop of Rochester, has to flee to the Frankish court when the locals revert to their old gods. Fortunately, Eadbald is persuaded to convert, as his father had done, a year after becoming king. But things go from bad to worse in London.

All three sons of Saeberht seem to agree to be joint kings: Sexred, Saeward and another son whose name we don't know. They keep to the old religion, preferring the gods they grew up with. Mellitus and his newfangled god aren't welcome in their kingdom. They chase him out of London and burn St Paul's cathedral. Mellitus flees back to Kent and then to Gaul with Justus of Rochester. The pope's plan for an Archbishopric in London is shelved. But Christianity in England – or Kent, at least – still needs a man in overall charge. Augustine was Bishop of Canterbury until his death in 604 and Laurence succeeds him, so the pope now promotes Laurence to Archbishop of Canterbury. Mellitus will have to be content until he eventually succeeds Laurence as archbishop. Justus also returns as Bishop of Rochester, the senior churchman in West Kent but subject to the Archbishop of Canterbury in East Kent.

In the year 625, the Roman Church has the opportunity to send one of its missionaries, Paulinus, to convert the people of Northumbria. His mission comes about when the King of Northumbria, Edwin, who rules from 616 to 632, wishes to marry a princess from

Did You Know?

Even centuries later, when various Bishops of London fell out with various Archbishops of Canterbury, the ancient plan of London being intended as the first archbishopric in England was often resurrected and thrown into the argument as a bit of one-upmanship.

Kent. The princess is Aethelburh, daughter of King Eadbald and granddaughter of Aethelberht. She was raised as a Christian of the Roman Church and her father isn't keen on her marrying a heathen like Edwin, although in 625 an alliance with Northumbria seems like an excellent idea because the Kingdom of Kent isn't quite as powerful as it was in Aethelberht's day. The two kings, Eadbald and Edwin, do a deal: Aethelburh can continue with her Christian worship after her marriage and will bring a missionary with her. It's agreed that Edwin will hear what the missionary has to say but makes no promise to abandon his heathen gods.

King Edwin isn't convinced. Then, at Easter 626, someone tries to assassinate him and the shock sends Aethelburh into premature labour with her first baby. Paulinus prays fervently to his Christian God and the king, his wife and newborn daughter, Eanflaed, survive. Paulinus explains that because of his prayers, God has preserved the royal family. Edwin is suitably impressed and allows his daughter and a group of courtiers to be baptised. He even agrees to his own baptism, if Paulinus's God helps him find and be revenged upon whoever sent the would-be assassin. However, when the guilty party is discovered and killed, God having kept his part of the deal, Edwin is in no hurry to fulfil his side of the agreement. In 627, Paulinus persuades the king to summon all the notables of his kingdom to discuss the matter. This great gathering happens just outside York and results in a mass baptism of both Edwin and his people. Coifi is probably one of the notables [see above].

Paulinus is given the freedom to go where he likes, between Lincoln and Hadrian's Wall, preaching his Roman faith and baptising anyone who wishes to become Christian. He works his socks off, converting the heathens and founding churches. Edwin promises him he can be Archbishop of York but just before he reaches this pinnacle of achievement, things turn ugly. In the year 632, the pagan king, Penda of Mercia – Northumbria's neighbouring kingdom to the south – invades Edwin's lands. Battle is joined, Edwin is slain

Anglo-Saxon carving of a king and queen at St Mary the Virgin's Church, Wirksworth, Derbys.

and Penda and his army go on the rampage. All Paulinus's efforts to bring Christianity to the Northumbrians are destroyed as he is forced to flee back to Kent, bringing the now-widowed Aethelburh and her children to safety in the south.

With Edwin dead, two hot-headed rivals, Osric and Eanfrith fight it out in 633, hoping to become King of Northumbria. Neither succeeds as Penda of Mercia watches and waits upon events.

As a sad little coda for Paulinus, the pope has sent him the gift of a fine pallium to celebrate his enthronement as Archbishop of York, unaware of the disasters unfolding. Instead, Paulinus does get the less exalted job as Bishop of Rochester back in Kent and will eventually be rewarded with sainthood.

Anglo-Saxon carving of a local lead miner known as 'T'Owd Man' at St Mary the Virgin's Church, Wirksworth, Derbys.

Despite these changes in fortune for Christianity, it's the royal women who keep it going in these early days, spreading the Word to the kingdoms of their new husbands, setting up and retiring to abbeys when widowed or if married life no longer appeals to them. These powerful women play a prominent role in the new religion as patrons of monasteries, supporting individuals who train for the priesthood and finding placements for them. Anglo-Saxon noblewomen take an active part in every aspect, even though they cannot be priests themselves. What they learn as children about running estates and households, they carry over into their roles as abbesses and prioresses. They are business women in every sense, managing people and resources, dealing with PR issues and communication throughout England and across Christian Europe, even sending missionaries, or going in person, to their ancestral homelands to convert their heathen cousins. If you're a woman of ambition, the Church may have a job for you.

An alternative to Rome's religion

If you're not happy with Woden and his fellow gods but some aspects of Augustine's and Paulinus's preaching don't appeal, is there a third alternative? Yes, you're in luck because Northern England has missionaries at work once more but this time they aren't sent by the pope. Instead, they are Irish monks from Iona and this is the Celtic Church's version of Christianity which has some subtle differences from that of Rome.

The Celtic form of Christianity was here at least a century and a half before the Romans took up the new faith in AD 323, when Christians were still being fed to the lions for the crowd's entertainment. It's not certain exactly when or how the earliest known Christians came to Britannia but it's thought that a British king, Lucius, was baptised in the faith at his own request, followed by many of his people, in the later second century. As written evidence, the early Church Father,

Tertullian, noted in AD 208 that parts of Britain inaccessible to the Romans are already conquered by Christ. Alban, Britain's first martyr, was executed in 305 for shielding a monk during a period of fervent persecution of Christians. This was just two decades before the Roman Empire was forced to adopt that same religion by the newly-converted Emperor Constantine and the Roman Church came into existence.

So the Celtic Church is much older than the Roman but was pushed to the outer edges of the empire by the newer version, mainly into Ireland where Roman sandals never trod but also in the little kingdom of Hwicca, near Worcester[5]. This earlier form of Christianity seems to have a much closer relationship with nature, probably because Celtic pagan worship was all about revering hills, springs, water courses, trees and woods and this carries over to colour the belief in one God as the Creator. They believe that mankind has inherited the Earth and is entrusted with its care, living in harmony with all nature. Nature is also a constant reminder of God's power and generosity to mankind, not only in the present but in its history and its future and the Celtic Church must honour all aspects of this God-given Earth.

Don't these attitudes sound wonderful and so 'green'? You can see why the Celtic Church might appeal to farmers and humble folk, even to time-travellers from the twenty-first century. Forty years after Augustine was preaching in Southern England, a monk named Aiden from the monastery of Iona, an island off the west coast of Scotland, was invited by the King of Northumbria to come and preach Christianity to his heathen people. Iona was a community of Irish monks and the king, Oswald, had lived with them when exiled from Northumbria in his youth and been baptised into the Celtic Church. [Edwin, Oswald's uncle, had become king after Oswald's father's death.] When Oswald becomes King of Northumbria in 634, after Osric and Eanfrith have destroyed each other, leaving the situation vacant, he asks the monks to send a missionary to reconvert the heathens in his kingdom.

The first man sent from Iona is a disaster, upsetting the people whom, he declares, are too stubborn to listen and be converted.

His replacement is Aiden who gets on well with his old friend Oswald and takes a gentler approach in preaching Christianity. Aiden strolls from village to village, getting to know the people and chatting about their lives, labours and difficulties, gradually introducing his religion as a possible solution to their problems and, if not, there is always the promise of eternity in Heaven as their reward for worshipping God.

Oswald gives Aiden the island of Lindisfarne, just off the coast and connected to the mainland by a causeway at low tide, as the seat of his bishopric. Oswald's favourite residence of Bamburgh Castle – named 'Bebba' after a Northumbrian queen – is close by so they can visit each other. Aiden brings other monks from Iona to Lindisfarne – known as Holy Island – and their little community becomes the centre of not only their missionary work but of religious book production. Books and literacy are new ideas to the Anglo-Saxons but Lindisfarne will be famous for them as well as thriving as a seat of learning.

But do you remember the pagan king, Penda of Mercia? He hasn't gone away and still has his eye on Northumbria and in 642 it's time to strike again at another weedy, soft-centred Christian rival: Oswald.

Penda's Mercian army ravages the countryside, marching to Bamburgh, Oswald's royal city. Finding he can't storm the well-defended city and doesn't have the equipment nor resources to besiege it, Penda sets the place on fire, using wood from demolished villages to set it ablaze. The smoke and flames are so great that Aiden sees the fire from Lindisfarne.

A page showing the Incipit to the Gospel of Matthew in the Lindisfarne Gospels.

Fortunately, the tide is out and he hurries across the causeway to help Oswald. Raising his hands and eyes to Heaven, Aiden calls God's attention to the evil thing Penda has done and straightaway God changes the wind direction. The flames now engulf Penda's men and the pagans flee, realising Bamburgh is protected by Aiden and his God. But Oswald's troubles with the Mercians are not over. Later that year, he faces them across the battlefield, probably near Oswestry, and is killed. But, godly to the last, it's said he dies praying for his men as the Mercians chop him up. No wonder Oswald and Aiden are both made saints.

Celtic or Roman? – The religious debate is settled

Oswald's younger brother, Oswiu, succeeds him as King of Northumbria and needs a wife. He looks no further than his cousin, Eanflaed, his Uncle Edwin's daughter who had been taken to safety in Kent with her mother, Aethelburh, by Paulinus, as you may remember. Perhaps Oswiu's and Eanflaed's marriage is a happy one but family disagreements are unavoidable. A big issue between them arises every Easter. Queen Eanflaed, raised in the Roman Church, is celebrating the Easter festival with a slap-up dinner with all the trimmings and shouting joyful 'Allelujahs', while King Oswui, baptised into the Celtic Church, is still wearing sackcloth and ashes and fasting for Lent. Some years, it's the other way around. This nightmare for the royal priests and cooks is caused because the two churches use different methods to calculate the date of Easter. Impossible! Something has to be done. A synod is held to debate the pros and cons and resolve the matter.

A synod is a meeting of bishops, abbots – and in this case an abbess as well – and any other high-ranking lay persons, like kings and queens, to discuss religious matters. Abbess Hild[a] of Whitby on the coast of Yorkshire offers her abbey as a suitable venue. It's a 'double'

Did You Know?

Celtic double houses allowed monks and nuns to 'come together' to produce the next generation of monks and nuns. The Roman Church wasn't keen on this style of worshipping God.

house – popular with the Celtic Church and having both monks and nuns – so can accommodate men and women without embarrassment.

The Synod of Whitby is held in 664 to sort things out[6]. Abbess Hild[a], raised in the Celtic Church, nevertheless supports Wilfrid, an Irish monk who trained in Rome and is spokesman for the Roman Church. The current Bishop of Lindisfarne, Colman, and monks from Iona speak for the Celtic Church. But Wilfrid is a brilliant wordsmith, arguing that Rome's way must be the way St Peter worked out Easter and Peter was appointed by Christ to set up the Church. Therefore, since Peter's method must be correct, Rome's must be also. This

Exterior of the Anglo-Saxon church of All Saints, Brixworth, Northants.

argument also applies to the Roman style of tonsure for priests and monks – a central shaved patch as opposed to a shaved forehead, not that either makes much difference to elderly balding churchmen – and any differences in the form of worship.

King Oswiu has the final word and, as a man of the Celtic Church, his decision is surprising. He finds in favour of Rome. Wilfred's silver tongue wins the day and he's another saint in the making. Bishop Colman of Lindisfarne is out of a job and he and his fellow monks of the Celtic persuasion go back to Iona. Rome prefers there to be an Archbishop of York, since the post was founded by their missionary, Paulinus [also a saint], and celebrate their success by immediately appointing Chad to that office. When he dies in 669, their favourite spokesman, Wilfrid, succeeds him. From now on, the Roman Church is unassailable and Oswiu and Eanflaed can happily celebrate Easter together.

Interior of All Saints Church, Brixworth, Northants, showing the Anglo-Saxon arches in the nave and side aisles [GRM 2023].

Chapter 5

Language and the Law

One of the first things you'll notice when, as a time-traveller, you arrive in Anglo-Saxon England is that the people speak a language which sounds nothing like modern English. If you understand German, there may be a few more similarities in the sound of the language but, even so, it's quite different. They are speaking Old English, a West Germanic language used in England between the fifth and twelfth centuries. The people call their language *Aenglisc,* [pro. Enn-glish] and their home is *Aengelcynn* or *Englaland.*

But across the land, the language may sound different because – as you'll remember – there are now Angles, Saxons, Jutes, Frisians, Swedes and maybe other groups from Europe, not forgetting the Roman Britons who are already here, all having various dialects and different words for the same thing. And then the Vikings arrive to add to the mix but more on them later. Yet they all need to communicate with each other.

Up until the coming – or reintroduction – of Christianity, *Aenglisc* is almost entirely a spoken language. If a stone marker or piece of craftwork needs to be inscribed with a name – as we saw with Tatberht and Oethilward of Lundenwic in Chapter 2 – then runic lettering is used. Runes consist mainly of straight lines so they're easy to carve and the alphabet, known as 'futhorc' and originating in Frisia, has up to thirty-three letters! Otherwise, there are no records, documents or stories written in *Aenglisc.*

Time immemorial

Every bit of information is remembered and the Anglo-Saxons must have phenomenal memories, which we know they do. In fact, writing is reckoned to be the lazy way of remembering things. When the monks introduce written records, the Anglo-Saxons often trust what is remembered rather than what is written down. They soon realise that what someone writes in ink on parchment may not be true or can be scraped off and changed. But what they say, face to face, you can question and argue with to get at the truth and test whether they're lying. They are suspicious of the written word and, perhaps, rightly so, on occasion.

In old legal documents, some written long after the Anglo Saxon period, you may see the phrase 'time immemorial'. This doesn't just mean 'long ago' but refers to a specific period of time which the oldest living person in the village can remember his or her grandparents or even great-grandparents mentioning. For example, perhaps someone's land boundary originally included an ancient oak tree which is long gone now but one of the villagers remembers her grandfather talking about climbing that tree as a lad, when it grew beside the little hillock where the church now stands. To the Anglo-Saxons, this passed-down memory has legal standing and is more trustworthy and believable than what some churchman or other has chosen to write and, possibly, 'adapt' to suit himself or his patron. The position of that tree, though no longer there, is still accepted as a valid boundary marker, perhaps to be reinstated with a new tree or a large stone which will remain in 'time immemorial' for future generations to recall.

Once the Christian missionaries arrive, whether Roman or Celtic, they swiftly introduce the art of writing to the unlettered Anglo-

Did You Know?

In the reign of King Edward the Confessor [1042-66], the monks at Westminster Abbey forged documents to enhance their royal connections and to lay claim to lands and properties that weren't legally theirs.

Saxons but all their documents are in Latin – the universal language of the Church across Europe. Since their homelands have never been part of the Roman Empire, other than the new churchmen, the Anglo-Saxons don't understand Latin, so any preaching, Bible readings or Gospel stories have to be translated into English. This can be done verbally as the missionaries learn the local dialect but, as we know, learned monks like to write things down and this is where the difficulties begin. The Anglo-Saxons have sounds in their speech which don't occur in Latin and Latin has letters which aren't required in Old English. Latin has 'v' but the Anglo-Saxons always use the softer 'f', at least until they began to adopt some Latin words into their everyday speech, so there is no 'v' in the Old English alphabet. In the early days, there isn't much use for 'k' either as 'c' is always pronounced as in 'cat'.

But English does have sounds not used in Latin for which extra letters had to be invented. The most frequently used sound which is unknown to Latin is 'th' in both its hard and soft forms: hard as in 'the' and 'there'; soft as in 'three' and 'heath'. The hard form is represented by 'eth' written as ð, and the soft by 'thorn', written as þ. And if you've always wondered why, in UK English, the word 'plough' is pronounced 'plow', you can blame that on the Old English letter 'g' which can be pronounced as 'g' in god, 'w' in bow or 'y' in day.

There are two more sounds used by the Anglo-Saxons which aren't used in Latin and so need letters to represent them. The first is 'w'

Did You Know?

Eth eventually came to be written like Y. The *y* in *ye* actually comes from eth which slowly merged with 'y' over time. In the beginning, *ye* was meant to sound the same as *the* but the incorrect spelling and mispronunciation live on in 'Ye Olde Tea Shoppe' and other such nonsense.

represented by 'wynn' and written as ƿ. But later 'uu' becomes more common, literally two 'u's. The other sound is the one which seems you need to cough – which is an example – the sound at the end of the Scottish loch or the composer Bach. It's known as 'yogh', written as ȝ. It's still visible as 'gh' in modern English but usually silent as in bought and daughter.

But understanding spoken Old English is likely to be easier for you than reading it because the letter 'c' is another tricky one. 'Cyning' is 'king' and that's how the word is said pretty much; 'cild' is child and sounds as you expect it should. So do 'scip' = ship; 'brycg' = bridge; 'cirice' = church and 'ceap' = cheap and actually means 'goods for sale'. Names ending in 'ic', such as Aelfric, are pronounced 'Aelfritch'.

Speaking of Aelfric, you must have noticed by now, throughout this little guide, how many names begin with and contain 'ae' together, such as Aethelberht and Aelfred [Alfred], who we'll meet later. This 'ae' [known as ash] is called a diphthong – there is also 'oe' [known as ethel] – where both vowels are sounded but run together smoothly [ae as in gate and oe as in oil]. Often, later, the diphthong becomes simply 'a' or sometimes 'e' or even reversed as in a word we met earlier, the Old English word for a pagan: 'haethen', which my auto-correct keeps changing to 'heathen'. Also, if there's an 'e' at the end of a word, it's pronounced – no wasted letters in Old English.

Once you've got the pronunciation straight in your mind, the difficulties don't end there because Old English has male, female and neuter genders in words and is an inflected language which means the words change according to the meaning. For example *se cyning lufath,* or the king loves, becomes *se cyning lufode,* the king loved in the past tense. The intricacies of Old English are too complicated for this short book but there are 'teach yourself' guides available[1].

One interesting word you'll need to know, if you get hungry, is *hlaf.* This means 'loaf', the 'h' is sounded softly [and eventually dropped], followed by 'laaff', and this is how the Anglo-Saxons refer to bread and to food generally. Surprisingly, *hlaf* has other uses too. The head of the household is the *hlaf-weard* or loaf-warden and anyone who eats the food is a *hlaf-aeta.* The lady of the house is the *hlaef-dige* or loaf-kneader, using the feminine form and where *dige* becomes our modern 'dough'. *Hlaf-weard* evolves, losing 'h' and 'f', running the words together so it sounds like 'lahrd, then the Scots 'laird' and, ultimately, 'lord'. So that grand title originally meant the guy in charge of the food[2]. *Hlaef-dige* goes through similar changes, dropping letters and with 'g' pronounced as 'y', to become 'lady'.

Writing it down

Kings quickly appreciate the idea of writing things down, even if their subjects can't see the point. If you invent a law code with hundreds of clauses, it's going to be hard to remember the details accurately, even for an Anglo-Saxon with a prodigious memory. The Kings of Kent aren't only the first to convert to Christianity, they're the first to take up the idea of having their laws recorded for posterity, which is marvellous for historians, if less so for the ne'er-do-wells of the day, and it means the law can be applied consistently throughout the realm. Since, as a time-traveller, you'll need to abide by these laws – remember, even in the twenty-first century, ignorance of the law doesn't get you off the hook if you break it – let's think about possible crimes you need to be aware of.

Perhaps for you, as a 'foreigner' – that doesn't necessarily mean you're from a distant land but rather that you're unknown to the locals – the most important thing is to announce your presence to the

---

♪ Top Tip

Only the most important religious buildings might have glass in the windows. Even kings' halls only have wooden shutters to cover the open windows and keep out the weather.

villagers. Shouting or blowing a horn are acceptable methods and must be done as soon as you leave the main road, according to the law code of King Wihtraed of Kent in 695. If you fail to tell everyone you've arrived, any crimes committed in the area will be reckoned as *your* doing, so make as much noise as you can if you don't want to be wrongly accused. Hedge-breaking is a common crime – we would call it breaking-and-entering [in daylight] or burglary [after dark]. It refers to somebody entering someone else's property without using the proper entrance, e.g., by busting down the hedge or fence or climbing through a window.

But, if you're caught 'red-handed' – literally referring to having blood still on your hands – the consequences can be extremely serious for you and expensive.

The earliest 'dooms' or law-codes – doom in the sense of judgement day – once they've made certain you know the Church is most important, even above the king, are all about *wergild* or man-payment. Before the Anglo-Saxons settled down quietly to farm the land, they were a quarrelsome and blood-thirsty people. Tit-for-tat blood feuds could go on for generations, so *wergild* is invented to stop this. Every man, woman, child and slave has a monetary value. Even a fingernail has a price. So, if a man injures you, instead of

---

Did You Know?

The earliest written Anglo-Saxon laws come from Kent, in the reign of King Aethelberht, c.600 AD, and are recorded in the early twelfth-century *Textus Roffensis,* kept at Rochester Cathedral. They were originally written in Old English and the scribe copied them into the textus precisely, using the same Kentish dialect of Old English as in Aethelberht's day, so some ancient words and grammar are found only here in the law code and nowhere else. By the way, 'textus' is the Latin word for a posh book with a decorated cover, perhaps jewelled and gilded, intended to be on display near the altar in a cathedral. A lesser, plain book is termed 'liber'.

The *Textus Roffensis* in Rochester Cathedral, Kent.

'an eye for an eye' or whatever damage he's done, he must pay you compensation, according to the 'doom' list. If he steals from you, he must pay you the value of what he took, plus a generous bonus for causing you inconvenience. If the criminal flees and can't be found, his kinsmen have to pay. If neither the criminal nor his relatives can afford to pay you in goods or money, either he or a kinsman must become your slave to work off the debt for a set term. Very civilised, isn't it? Sadly, as Christianity becomes more powerful in England, capital punishment gradually replaces *wergild*, which is unfortunate because a hanged man does his victim no good at all, whereas compensation can be extremely helpful.

Here are the first clauses in Aethelberht's doom list, dealing with stealing church property:

1. God's property and the church's *[is to be compensated]* with 12-fold compensation.
2. A bishop's property with 11-fold compensation.
3. A priest's property with 9-fold compensation.
4. A deacon's property with 6-fold compensation.
5. A cleric's property with 3-fold compensation.

But then:
10. If a freeman should steal from the king, let him compensate with 9-fold compensation.

So the king is equal to a priest but less than a bishop[3].

Whatever you do, try to avoid getting involved in fisticuffs of any kind. Trust me, you can't afford it. And, if the worst does happen in a fight, no distinction exists between intentional murder and accidental manslaughter: dead is dead and the victim's family must receive the appropriate *wergild*. In a later law-code of King Aelfred: the price for killing an ealderman or noble is 300 shillings; for killing a churl or a freeman is 100 shillings. And clause 77 deals with the possibility of severe injury which doesn't cause death: 'If a man ruptures the tendons on another's neck and wounds them so severely that he has no power over them, and lives despite such wounding, let 100 shillings be given him as compensation, unless the Witan decrees to him a greater and more just compensation.' The Witan, the king's council, can increase the *wergild* at its discretion, perhaps depending upon the degree of paralysis the victim suffers.

But returning to Aethelberht's law-code, these are the costs if you inflict a lesser wound or what you will receive, if you are injured by another:

53. If a person strikes off a thumb, 20 shillings.
54. If a thumbnail becomes off, let him pay 3 shillings.

55. If a person strikes off a shooting finger *[a forefinger]*, let him pay 9 shillings.
56. If a person strikes off a middle finger, let him pay 4 shillings.
57. If a person strikes off a goldfinger *[a ring finger which is considered to have a direct connection to the heart, so is thought more important]*, let him pay 6 shillings.
58. If a person strikes off the little finger, let him pay 11 shillings. *[Not sure why a little finger is even more valuable.]*
59. For each of the nails, a shilling.
60. For the least disfigurement of the appearance, 3 shillings. And for the greater, 6 shillings.
61. If a person strikes another in the nose with his fist, 3 shillings.

[It might almost be worth losing a couple of fingernails, if you're short of cash?]

You will also incur financial penalties for illicit sex with the lord's cup-bearer [usually his wife, daughter or female relative], his grinding slave [the girl who grinds the corn into flour] or any other female slaves, with payment paid to the lord, according to his and the woman's rank. You mustn't force an unwilling widow to marry you, either, else that'll cost you, according to her rank.

There's no such thing as equality here. If a woman has sex with a man, *he* pays, even if it was her idea. And there are no charges brought if a woman 'forces' a widower to marry her. It just doesn't happen in Anglo-Saxon society where men are men… and you know the rest.

Regarding property, owning land is down to an agreement made on two sides. It's a verbal contract and lapses if one party dies. For your ordinary Anglo-Saxon, this means that his or her heirs have to renegotiate the deal with the overlord when they die and the same applies if the lord dies. However, the Church likes to know exactly where it stands on matters of owning land and property and, unlike mortal individuals, it isn't going to die, so a verbal contract which ends with death isn't good enough. As we've seen, churchmen insist on writing things down, preferably in a large book that isn't likely to be mislaid or lost. Kings see this as a good idea as well and begin to have their property deals set down in writing. The estates that are recorded become known as *bocland;* that is 'bookland', the origin of the English 'freehold' system of land tenure.

Why is England unique?

The Anglo-Saxon dooms make English law unique. Across Europe, other societies which were once part of the Roman Empire keep their Roman laws, which include the idea that the accused is guilty unless he can prove himself innocent. But England's laws are turned upside down by the Anglo-Saxons who were never under Roman jurisdiction. Their ideas include, as we've seen, the payment of cash compensation or service, rather than executing the guilty. Also, the accused is presumed innocent until proven guilty, switching the burden of proof from the defendant to the prosecution. Fortunately, in later centuries, this form of the law, known as Common Law, was shipped out by the British to her Colonies across the world which still base their constitutions and rights on these Anglo-Saxon ideas, mostly, except for *wergild* which should be re-introduced, if anyone asks me.

Common Law doesn't mean it's a cheap thing found everywhere. In this case 'common' refers to the common folk. Supposedly, it's the law as determined by the ordinary people. It's not Church [or Canon] Law nor Roman Law as imposed by the Senate and, later, the emperor in Rome. Officially, the king draws up the code after discussing it with his Witan members who discuss it with their underlings, so it's all very democratic. This probably isn't often the case but we do know King Aethelberht summoned his under-kings, Saeberht of Essex and Raedwald of East Anglia, to a council meeting or two. They probably exchange gifts as well as ideas on keeping law and order in their kingdoms.

Another aspect of Common Law is based on that most important thing: memory. What folk remember happening in the past, in 'time immemorial', is the foundation for the law, termed 'precedent'. Whenever a case comes to trial, even in the twenty-first century, it's all based on precedent which means the last time we had a case like this, we did so-and-so. Therefore, to be consistent, we follow the same procedure as we did then. This works brilliantly until there's a case like nothing ever before. Take cybercrimes, for example, when our Common Law is at a loss what to do. New legislation has to be passed which takes ages, by which time the criminals have moved on and invented a new crime. But at least, for the Anglo-Saxons, their technology – and therefore novelty crime – moves at the pace of an ox drawing a plough, so Common Law is perfectly adequate.

But there is another aspect to England's uniqueness – the way her language evolves. You may remember that Old English has male, female and neuter genders in words and it's an inflected language so words change according to their meaning, whether a noun is the subject or the object of a sentence, for example. Latin has six singular and six plural versions of a noun, depending on whether it's the subject or object, if it's being spoken to directly, or if it possesses something, is over, under or on something else or moving, etc. But in modern English, a table is a table, whatever position it has in a sentence and it has no gender so that's irrelevant to any adjective used to describe it. If you've studied most other European languages based on Latin, such as French, Spanish or Italian, you'll know how complicated they can be. Likewise, the Germanic languages, of which Anglo-Saxon is one, are equally tricky. I know modern English suffers from quirky, awkward spelling and a few irregular verbs, like 'to be' which is a nasty one, but the genders and declensions of nouns are gone. Why did Old English lose most of its inflections?

A lot of unpleasantness is often blamed on the Vikings but it's because of them that English has dropped many of its complications. There comes a time [see Chapter 7] when half of England is known as the Danelaw, as I'll explain later. Most of the eastern side of England is occupied by the Danes with their own language, laws and customs. They're no longer marauding Vikings but – mostly – peaceful,

> ## Did You Know?
>
> Whether you're <u>angry</u> with your <u>husband</u> or <u>give</u> him a <u>hug</u>, whether there is a <u>gale</u> blowing or <u>fog</u> outside, if you <u>give</u> a <u>guest</u> you don't <u>trust</u> a <u>kick</u> on the <u>leg</u> or <u>toss</u> him out the <u>window</u>, you can't do any of these things without using Old Danish words adopted into English. (Words of Danish origin are underlined).

settling down to farm the land and trade with their neighbours. But it's difficult to do business with people you can't understand and so a new language begins to evolve, incorporating both English and Danish words. The grammar of the two doesn't have a lot in common and genders clash so frequently – is a cartwheel masculine, feminine or neuter and does it really matter when you need yours mended, urgently? – that they are forgotten.

The language we call English today is actually a hybrid with thousands of Danish words, along with Latin from the Church, Norman French from William the Conqueror's gang, Hindi from the time Britain was big in India and a whole assortment of vocabulary from all over the world.

Sometimes, both the English and Danish words remain in use but take on slightly different meanings, for example, the Old English *scyrte* is a short, loose garment worn by men and women or as we say 'shirt'. But Old Danish has *skirt* to describe the same item of clothing which we now use for the longer lower half of a garment[4].

Anglo-Saxon Chronicles

Thank goodness the Anglo-Saxons took to writing things down – at least, the monks did – otherwise this period of our history really would be 'a dark age', relying on archaeology to tell the story and not much besides. But one difficulty for historians is that Christian monks have a skewed view of everyday life. Pagans automatically get a bad press – they can't possibly do anything vaguely worthy and good unless they convert to Christianity – and mundane daily activities, especially women's work, aren't of any interest and don't get a mention. For example, Edwin becomes King of Northumbria in 617 but, like the kings in the south, at first he prefers the old religion. Not until he is baptised can Edwin qualify as a Christian hero and Bede, the Northumbrian chronicler, can't praise the convert too highly. Let's ask Bede to tell us about Edwin:

'God bless you, Brother Bede.'

'God's blessings upon you also. I suppose you wish to know something of the history of our people? Why else would you interrupt my writing?'

'I want to know about King Edwin. He seems to be a favourite of yours.'

'Favourite? Aye, well he was in favour with our Lord Christ for the way he brought peace to his people. Edwin was England's fifth mighty king, the *Bretwalda,* ruling over lesser kings like an imperial emperor. He knew how to demonstrate his strength such that evil-doers feared him utterly. Of course, this was only when he had God's divine power at his back, after he was baptised. It was a pity it took him so long before he saw the light and received the Holy Word into his heart. But better late than never.'

'Tell us how Edwin showed his strength.'

'He showed it marvellously. Hear me on this. He would ride out with his ealdermen and thegns, banners unfurled in imperial array, putting the fear of God into all who saw him, such that none dared challenge his overlordship. In his day – after his conversion – he so imposed his protection and made everywhere safe and peaceable that a mother with her infant might travel, unescorted, anywhere in the kingdom and come to no harm. The weak and vulnerable had no need to fear, such was Edwin's righteous rule.'

'That sounds great. It's nice to feel safe.'

'Aye, and your valuables were safe too. All along the highways, wherever a spring or fresh water was close at hand, Edwin had the places marked, setting up stakes, each with a fine bronze cup hung there that travellers could take and use it to slake their thirst. And such was the people's devotion to and respect for their lord that none dared steal these valuable cups and keep them for their own.'

'So I supposed Edwin must have gone on to rule his peaceful kingdom for many years and died in his bed at a great age?'

'Mm.'

'Sorry? I didn't catch that. Did Edwin have a long and happy reign, ruling with God on his side?'

'Edwin must have erred in some way… offended against the Lord Christ.'

'Why? What happened?'

'Just five years of peace were shattered in AD632 when Edwin was slain in battle by King Penda of Mercia. Terrible. Our beloved Northumbria shattered into many little lordships, each barely worth a mention. Chaos and catastrophe!'

'I suppose God must have been on Penda's side, if he defeated Edwin so drastically?'

'He most certainly was not! That wretch Penda was a heathen, a worshipper of idols. God wouldn't support a pagan. Obviously.'

'And yet the pagan beat the Christian?'

'As I said, Edwin must have offended God in some way we know not. Now cease your foolish questions and go away. I have a history book of monumental importance to write for posterity.'

'Yes. I'll read it in a thousand years' time or so.'

'Don't be facetious, you young upstart. Pass me that new sheet of parchment before you go.'

Brother Bede, writing his *Ecclesiastical History of the English People* in his monastery in Jarrow in Northumbria, becomes known as 'The Venerable Bede' and famous in his own lifetime. He is born on the abbey lands in 672/3 and spends his childhood in the monastery. In 686, plague comes to Jarrow and kills the majority of the monks and people of the town but Bede and his guardian, Abbot Ceolfrith, are the sole survivors among the brethren and have to rebuild the monastery, bringing in new brothers and novices. He rarely leaves it, although he does visit other monasteries and goes to York on one occasion but Jarrow has an excellent library of 200 books to help him with his history. He becomes well known because he gathers information from anyone who passes through, like a modern journalist. And like a journalist, he makes a few mistakes, especially with dates, promotes Northumbria at every opportunity and sensationalises his stories, if it suits him to do so.

Remains of Bede's monastery at Jarrow, Tyne and Wear.

Bede also writes letters to many who send him information. Most of his knowledge about the Kingdom of Kent and the work of Augustine comes from Albinus, the Abbot of St Augustine's Abbey in Canterbury, and a London priest, Nothhelm, who has visited Rome and brought back copies of letters to and from Pope Gregory about the conversion of Kent to Christianity. Bishop Daniel of Winchester sends him information about the progress of Christianity and the Church in Wessex; Abbot Esi tells of the East Anglian Church and Bishop Cynibert supplies details about the sub-kingdom of Lindsey in the area of Lincoln. Bede acknowledges his sources which is useful for historians.

Altogether, Bede writes about sixty books, not all on history or directly about religion. He teaches mathematics as well and translates Latin and Greek texts into English to help his novices in their studies. Bede also helps posterity by encouraging the use of the *Anno Domini* dating system throughout Europe which is a huge help to historians. Previously, if dates were cited at all, it was in terms of the local king and how long he had reigned, so 'in the sixth year of King Edwin's reign', for example. This is fine, if you know about Edwin but if you live in Kent, how does this correspond to the reign of Eadbald or in East Anglia, to that of King Raedwald? The year numbering will be different in every kingdom and confusion must occur when kings come and go in quick succession or return to reign for a second time. So Bede's AD dating system is invaluable.

The monk is still writing in his fifty-ninth year, as he tells us, but he is ill – too sick to visit York for the grand occasion when the bishopric is raised to an archbishopric which it remains in the twenty-first century. Yet Bede continues to write from his bed, dictating to young Wilberht up to an hour or two before his last breath on Thursday 26 May AD735 – no matter which king is reigning that day.

A later set of records of huge importance to history is *The Anglo-Saxon Chronicle,* commissioned by King Aelfred towards the end of the ninth century. It is written in Old English and gives a year by year account of the history of the Anglo-Saxons using information taken from a range of sources – it's an early version of Wikipedia, you might say. Bede's history and other Northumbrian annals are used, along with the genealogies of the various royal families, including their legendary and mythological ancestors. A number of Anglo-Saxon kings claimed to be descended from Woden. Lists of kings and bishops provide further details, along with histories of Wessex itself.

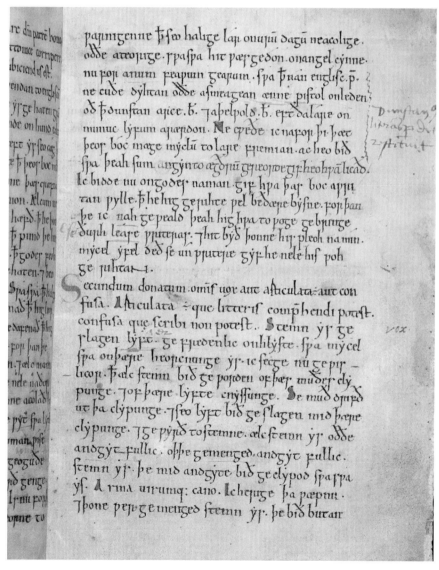

A page from Aelfric's *Grammar* in the British Library.

However, since King Aelfred ruled Wessex – a kingdom we haven't heard much about so far – the history begins with a pro-Wessex slant, unsurprisingly. After all, any king wants his people to be the heroes of the story. But copies of this official chronicle are then sent out to various monasteries and minsters across the land where local scribes continue to update them from their own point of view. The chronicle is still being kept in a few places even after the Norman Conquest, by which time local news bulletins make each version unique. Not all are accurate and, on some issues, neither is the original. Some scribes are sloppy about dates; others delight in recording hearsay, not bothered whether it's true. But whatever its failings, *The Anglo-Saxon Chronicle* is one of our best sources for the events in England in the later period, as we shall discover in further chapters of this little guide.

Did You Know?

Around 998, Aelfric of Eynsham produced a *Grammar*, written in Old English, designed to explain Latin. It's the earliest surviving textbook in English and has notes on all sorts of word constructions, including using 'haha' and 'hehe' to denote laughter in text: according to Aelfric, these were the same in English and Latin.[5]

Chapter 6

Health and Welfare

To you, as a traveller from the twenty-first century, health care is probably something you take for granted along with the wonders of modern medicine but how do the Anglo-Saxons deal with health-related matters? What happens if you're in need of medical advice or suffer an accident? There is no Accident and Emergency Department, no Emergency Room, so where can you go for help or are you a lost cause without hope?

Firstly, before you panic, it's helpful to know that the Anglo-Saxon diet is generally great for your health with no additives, artificial colourants, herbicides, fungicides or E-numbers.

Secondly, some diseases you might worry about don't exist in Anglo-Saxon England: measles, as I mentioned before, is believed to have evolved in the eleventh century. Cholera, syphilis [probably, though the advent of this disease in Europe is being re-thought] and many age-related ailments are rare because life is hazardous and only monks and nuns, tucked safely in their religious houses, tend to live beyond forty or fifty years.

On the other hand, leprosy, now known as Hansen's disease, is more common. Although leprosy is a terrible disease with no treatment

Did You Know?

After the Norman Conquest of 1066, a number of displaced Anglo-Saxons went to Constantinople where the Emperor was eager to have them join his personal bodyguard because they were taller than other nationalities, grown impressive and intimidating on the Anglo-Saxon diet.

known to the Anglo-Saxons, it comes in many guises, most of which aren't fatal. Because the early symptoms are somewhat similar in appearance to other common skin problems, like eczema, psoriasis and dermatitis, these can all be wrongly diagnosed as leprosy. Also, it isn't nearly as contagious as believed: you can't catch it if a leper breathes on you and many saintly folk work in leper hospitals for years without developing the illness. These places aren't hospitals as we think of them. They are more like isolated communities, known as Lazar houses because, in the Bible, Christ is said to have miraculously raised Lazarus from the dead after he died – maybe – from leprosy. The idea is to prevent the lepers coming into contact with healthy people and infecting them.

What if I feel unwell?

If you are unfortunate enough to become unwell or suffer an injury, you need to understand that the Anglo-Saxons, once they've converted to Christianity, regard God as the Universal Physician who can cure anything, if He wishes to. So, your cheapest and simplest medical treatment is prayer. You can pray for yourself, of course, and if you ask a priest, a monk or a nun to pray on your behalf, they'll expect a 'donation' of some kind but it's still the cheapest – and painless – treatment. If God thinks you're worthy of His attentions, you'll recover in no time but, if you've sinned, then illness is your deserved punishment as God teaches you to mend your ways. Suffering now, in this life, is better than the pains of Hell for all eternity. That's the way sickness is regarded.

However, the Anglo-Saxons like to keep their options open. Before Christianity arrived, numerous superstitions about how to remain safe and in good health were available and hands up – be honest now – who avoids walking under ladders or breathes a sigh of relief when Friday the thirteenth passes without some disaster? Superstitions are still with us in the twenty-first century. The Anglo-Saxons believe illness is caused by evil demons, bad spirits and especially elves. These aren't merry little fairy folk. Elves lurk in dark corners and hide in the shadows, armed with their tiny bows and arrows, waiting to shoot at unwary humans with their poisoned darts and make them unwell, enjoying their torment. You may have experienced this yourself if you've had watery-elf disease with its nasty, itchy, blister-type spots. It's the elves' favourite ailment to inflict on hapless mankind – today, we call it chicken pox.

To counter the elves and demons, charms and amulets are the thing. A miniature Thunor's [Thor's] hammer, perhaps carved from wood or horn, hung as a charm around your neck will not only ward

An amulet or charm will ward of disease and keep you safe.

off lightning strikes but scare away evil of many kinds. For double protection, keep a tiny scroll of parchment, written with Latin prayers, against your skin beneath your clothes for maximum security. Wear the charm and amulet constantly to ensure your health and wellbeing since you need the gods of every religion on your side in the fight against sickness and the wicked spirits which cause it.

If both your charm and amulet should fail – unlikely, obviously – and prayers don't bring about a rapid recovery, what is your next option?

Herbal treatments*

There are no trained physicians for the simple reason that there are no universities where they can study the knowledge and learn the skills required but do not despair. Without any official degrees and certificates, there are folk who can help you. If your village has one, the local wise woman knows which herbs can relieve your symptoms, where they grow and how best to preserve and prepare them as a treatment for you. Most remedies are 'simples', in other words they contain a single active ingredient. A tisane of selfheal [*Prunella vulgaris*] – also called heal-all and woundwort – made by pouring hot water over the plant in a cup and leaving it to steep [brew], will make you feel better, whatever your ailment. Binding it on an injury aids healing.

Comfrey [*Symphytum officionale*] is also known as knit-bone. The grated root is made into a poultice and sets hard like a plaster cast to help immobilise a broken bone or ease a sprain. The young leaves of the white-flowered – but not the blue-flowered – comfrey can be used as a vegetable with a unique flavour, good as batter-coated fritters, and the stems may be cooked and eaten like asparagus.

---

* These are just a few of the herbs available to the Anglo-Saxons as medical treatments but a word of caution: I have done my research into ancient herbal remedies and strongly advise you to seek expert help before trying any of them.

The word salve has come to mean a healing ointment of any kind or even something to soothe your feelings or your conscience but it originally meant a treatment made with sage [*Salvia officionalis*] – any plant with 'officionalis' in its Latin name has been used in medicine in the past. The plant came to England from the Mediterranean with the Romans but soon escaped the garden to grow wild. Sage mixed with goose grease is the original soothing ointment but sage is also reckoned to be good for the memory, hence wise old folk being known as sages.

Wild rose petals [*Rosa canina*], laid on the closed eyelids soothe sore eyes and the flesh of rosehips, de-pipped, de-haired and cooked with honey, is excellent for coughs and colds. We know this is because it contains lots of vitamin C – the Anglo-Saxons simply know it works but not why. Meadowsweet [*Filipendula ulmaria*] is brilliant for headaches, joint pain and reducing fevers. Its flowers are full of sweet honeyed nectar and it grows in damp places.

Many plants with a mint flavour, like common spearmint [*Mentha spicata*], are good for stomach upsets but best of all is another herb introduced by the Romans which has gone wild: camomile [*Matricaria chamomilia*]. Hopefully, your village wise woman will know where this little plant with its daisy-like flowers can be found because if drunk as a tisane it's a marvellous remedy for stomach cramps, indigestion, flatulence, nausea, vomiting, colic and diarrhoea.

One other wonderful herb, native to this country, is sweet cicely [*Myrrhis odorata*]. This plant has an aniseed flavour and, if drunk as a tisane, is a remedy for asthma and other breathing problems, coughs, throat and chest ailments, poor digestion and even urinary tract disorders. But even if you're perfectly fit and well, the whole plant is edible, even the root can be cooked or eaten raw. In this time before sugar, sweet cicely is a great sweetener with an aniseed flavour. The black seeds can be ground and used as a spice.

One herb I must mention because it's particularly important to the Anglo-Saxons is a bright yellow, large, spring-flowering daisy, elecampane [*Inula helenium*] but also known as horse-heal and elf-dock. Its roots are used to treat elfshot, if those pesky pixies get you with their nasty little arrows, leaving you feeling fatigued and exhausted. It's great for a pick-me-up and good for treating coughs and clearing the chest.

Medical matters

But some folk need more than a 'simple' to treat their ailments and if your appeals to God have been ignored then, like the unfortunate King Aelfred, you may have to consult a leech. This is a last resort because it's expensive and may do more harm than good but some Anglo-Saxon doctors have a few marvellous tricks up their sleeve.

King Aelfred [AD 871-99] suffers from a number of ailments including piles [haemorrhoids] which must be agonising if you have to spend so much time riding a horse. He is also tormented by a mysterious and debilitating pain which first afflicts him on his wedding night and plagues him for the rest of his days, although it doesn't prevent him fathering at least five children who live to become adults. So the king requires the services of a skilled *laech* [pro. leech] and, fortunately Bald, a monk, is one of the best. Well, a king can afford the cost, can't he?

Bald is not only good at his job; very thoughtfully he has a scribe named Cild [pro. chilled] record all his treatments and remedies in *The Leechbook of Bald* so we can read about his methods today[1]. He includes Greek and Roman recipes as well as those given him

Did You Know?

Those slug-like leeches, so popular with doctors back through history and still used today if you require a digit to be sewn back on, got their name from the Anglo-Saxon word for a physician, *laech*.

by fellow Anglo-Saxon physicians, Oxa and Dun. There are surgical treatments to fix a hare lip and a cleft palate, charms for dealing with those pesky elves, cures for lust and impotence and diagnostic techniques, mostly written in Old English with some Latin when the Anglo-Saxon language doesn't have a suitable word. Let's ask Bald about his book:

'God bless you, Brother Bald. Excuse us interrupting but could you tell us about the leechbook Cild is writing for you? How useful is it?'

'Well, it ought to be very helpful to my fellow medical men and women, both now and in the future. Why are you interested?'

'I'm, er, writing a book, too. I see you're preparing something in that pot over the fire.'

'That's for treating the king's piles. They're tormenting him today. I'm steeping oak bark and leaves, infusing them in hot water. It's a good treatment for piles but also for ulcers, over-loose bowels, tumours, swelling and bleeding. More than that, oak promotes healing, brings down fevers and is a most excellent antidote to poison. You must include that in your book, if it's about medical matters?'

'I touch on health issues…'

'Then note this down… come along… where's your stylus and tablet, eh? For dimness of eyes... take bright celandine flowers, mix with bumble bee's honey and warm it over a fire – don't boil it, or it'll be ruined. This removes film and spots from the surface of the eyes. What are you squinting at? Perhaps you need this remedy yourself?'

'No. I was wondering if it does any good?'

'Of course it does, as does my ointment for treating a sty on the eyelid but that requires a number of ingredients and complex preparation, so I'll give you the recipe in writing later, if you wish it.'

'Thank you, brother, but I know something of this remedy already. It's a wonderful antibiotic.'

'An anti-what?'

'Er, an anti-elf potion, you might say. What's going on there? That looks like liver?'

'It is, from a buck. That too is a treatment for eyes – night blindness, in this case. The patient must eat of the liver night and morn.'

'That would work because liver contains vitamin A.'

'Viterminay? What is that?'

'No matter, it hasn't been discovered yet.'

'You speak in riddles. Now don't forget to explain in your book about the significance of the number nine.'

'Number nine? What of it?'

'You must use it in healing rituals. Charms and prayers must be repeated nine times in order to be most effective. When mixing a salve or a remedy it must be stirred nine times and others should be left to stand for nine days to become most potent, like that sty remedy I promised you. Oh, see, the oak treatment is ready now for Lord Aelfred. I must go to him.'

'I hope it works.'

'Of course it will.'

'I wanted to ask you more about elves…'

'No time now. Farewell.'

Brother Bald was most helpful, wasn't he? All the remedies he mentioned might well be effective, though I hear he uses pigeon dung occasionally. Who knows what that's supposed to do? But he has sent us his remedy for a sty on the eye:

> *Take cropleek and garlic, of both equal quantities,*
> *pound them well together, take wine and bullocks' gall,*
> *of both equal quantities, mix with the leek, put this then*
> *into a brazen vessel, let it stand nine days in the brass*

Did You Know?

In 2015, scientists at Nottingham University recreated this recipe, using onion, garlic, cow's bile and wine, all mixed in a brass bowl and left it to stand for nine days, as instructed. They were astonished at how effective it was as an antibiotic, wiping out cultures of the superbug MRSA. Further investigation of Bald's remedy goes on.

vessel, wring out through a cloth and clear it well, put it into a horn, and about night time apply it with a feather to the eye.

Bald's *Leechbook* doesn't have much to say about surgery but from archaeological evidence found on Anglo-Saxon skeletons, we know they are skilled at splinting broken bones and carry out successful operations of trepanation – that is drilling out a section of the skull. The idea is to let the worm/elf/demon escape which is causing a serious headache but, in cases of concussion, easing the pressure on the brain by this method can be a life-saver. Some skulls have been found which show a trepanation that has healed, so recovery is possible. Surgery on haemorrhoids is also practised but maybe Aelfred doesn't trust his doctors that far as it's quite gruesome. Wounds are sewn with silk thread which dissolves away slowly, so no need to remove the stitches. Doctors also know about packing large wounds with sphagnum moss and smearing cuts with honey. Without knowing it, they are applying antiseptic, antibiotic treatments, but they understand that these things aid healing and reduce the likelihood of infection and sepsis.

Bald's *Leechbook* also contains a recipe for a treatment for burns which is quite simple and can be made in a pot over the fire, mixing woad with butter. Woad is used to dye cloth blue. Although the flowers are yellow, the root when mashed up and exposed to the air turns blue. Mixed with butter to make it into a creamy consistency and applied to burns and scalds, the blue colour reflects ultra-violet light,

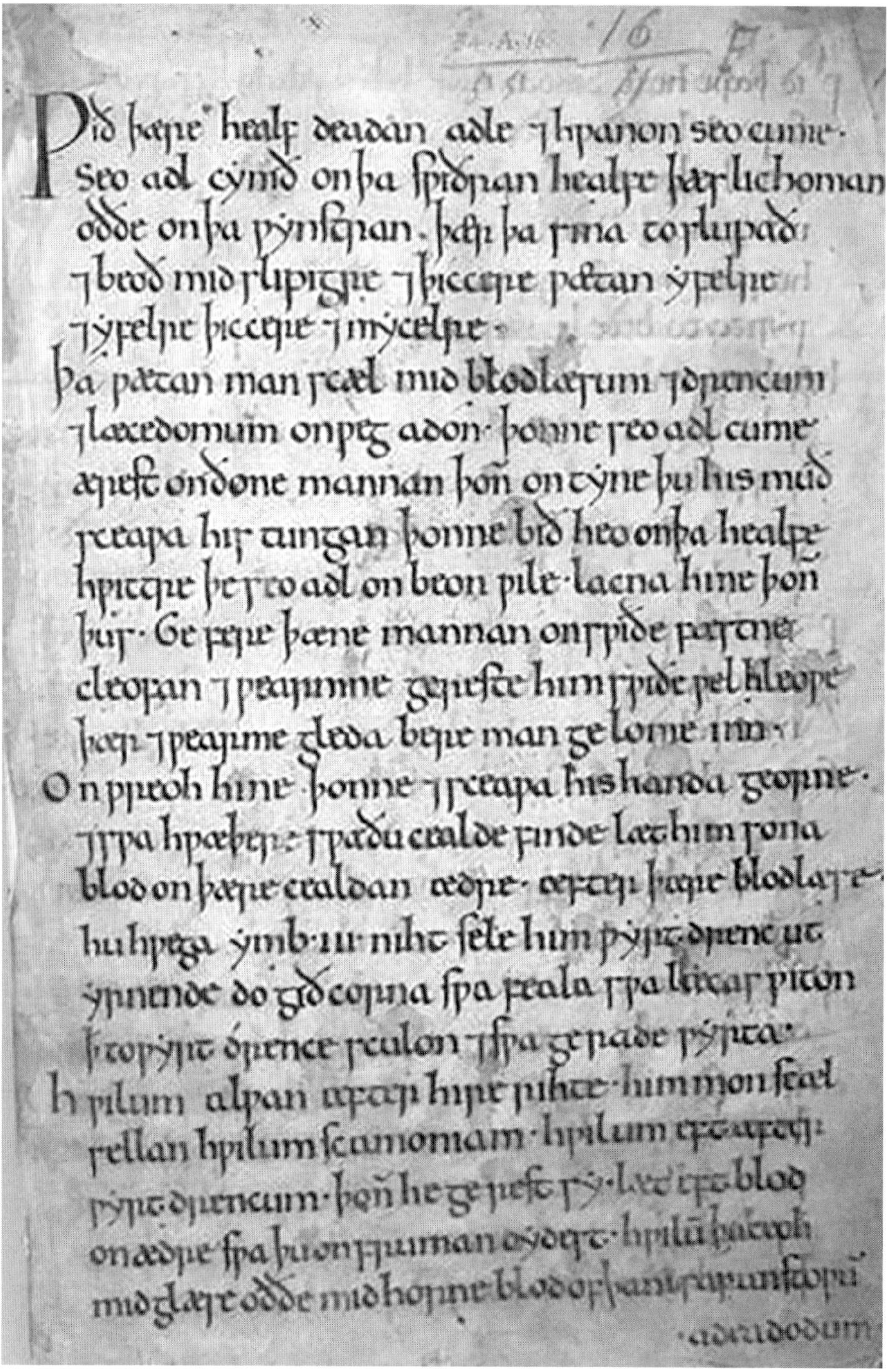

The Leechbook of Bald.

reducing blistering, while the butter sooths the injury and keeps out the air. Bald also has a recipe for easing muscle aches and pains made from stinging nettles. In the twenty-first century, similar ointments are commercially available. Obviously, Bald knows a thing or two about easing pain and discomfort.

Minsters

In the twenty-first century, England still has a number of place names involving the word 'minster', Westminster and York Minster being the most well-known. Dorset has quite a collection including Beaminster, Charminster, Wimbourne Minster and Yetminster. Devon has Axminster, Exminster, Sturminster Marshall and Sturminster Newton. From Northumberland to the Welsh border, Somerset to Essex; minsters are found all over England and who can say how many have been lost to history. But what is a minster?

The dictionary tells us it's a religious house, an important church or the church which serves a monastic community. But for the Anglo-Saxons a minster is much more than that. Minsters are the forerunners of cathedrals, abbeys and parish churches, serving the purposes of all three. Sometimes they are 'duel houses' of both monks and nuns, though the two sexes are kept well apart and celibate, unlike the double houses of the Celtic Church. Other minsters are centres for secular priests who go out into the community, preaching, conducting services, baptising, etc. The point of a minster is that it 'administers' the local area, rather like the later parish churches, but covering a far larger range. Ministers act as lords of the manor but, unlike kings and thegns who move around, they are stationary so, provisions, taxes due, court cases and fines have to come to the minsters.

In return, the minsters serve as a community hub, providing not just spiritual care but physical care and welfare. As we've seen, the physicians and surgeons of the day, like Bald, are monks and priests.

> **🔖 Top Tip**
> _____
>
> Easing your pain and caring for your body are of secondary importance since suffering on earth improves your soul's chances of a place in heaven.

Nuns too are often skilled herbalists and apothecaries, growing medicinal plants in the minster garden or collecting them from the woods, meadows and hedgerows. Minsters usually have an infirmary attached, although treatment there is more about tending your soul and preparing it for the inevitable end.

The majority of minsters are royal foundations, set up by charters, granted estates by bookland [see Chapter 5] and having special rights and privileges. Minsters are excused the services due from other land-holders, such as providing men and weapons in time of war, and aren't required to pay taxes to the king either. So, what benefit does a king get from founding a minster? The primary benefit is to his soul as the monks, nuns and priests are obliged to pray constantly for their founder's spiritual well-being. Secondly, they provide excellent business opportunities for unwed princesses and widowed queens as well as educational establishments for training future bishops and young noblewomen destined for political marriages or to become nuns and even abbesses.

Minster-in-Sheppey, Kent

In case you think the life of an Anglo-Saxon nun might suit you – and it's certainly the best way for a girl to get an education – let's look at the story of one minster. Minster on the Isle of Sheppey, just off the north coast of Kent, is a royal foundation, set up around AD670 by the widowed queen Seaxburh. She is the daughter of King Anna of East Anglia [slain by Penda of Mercia in 654] and weds Eorcenberht,

King of Kent, grandson of Aethelberht, Augustine's first royal convert to Christianity, although Eorcenberht prefers to worship Woden and the old gods. After his death in 664, having served as regent for her young son, Ecgberht, until he is old enough to rule, Seaxburh founds

St Seaxburh's Chapel, Minster-in-Sheppey, Kent.

a nunnery on Sheppey – the Isle of Sheep. Perhaps she hopes to improve her husband's standing with the new God by praying for his wayward soul, She endows the new minster with her own estates to provide an income and becomes its first abbess, overseeing seventy-seven nuns, one of whom is her daughter, Eormenhild, a widow, having been married to Wulfhere, King of Mercia.

There is no stone suitable for building on the island so materials are quarried at Boughton Monchelsea in Kent and brought down the River Medway to Sheppey. Examples of early Anglo-Saxon stonework and Roman tiles from the garrison fort at Reculver can still be found in the walls of the Chapel of St Seaxburh in the twenty-first century and three of the minster's wells still exist and function by the gatehouse, under a shop in Minster High Street and another in the garden of a house adjacent.

In 675, Seaxburh has a dream or a vision in which she sees the death of her sister, Abbess Aethelthryth of Ely. Seaxburh rushes off to Ely, leaving Eormenhild as abbess in her place at Minster. In Ely, she has her sister's saintly remains reburied in a marble tomb instead of the original wooden coffin and takes over as Abbess of Ely. When Seaxburh foresees her own death, she makes arrangements to be buried beside Aethelthryth. Both women are made saints and Seaxburh becomes the patron saint of her earlier foundation at Minster-in-Sheppey, together with St Mary the Virgin. After her mother's death, Eormenhild, described as 'the handmaid of God… [who] by her sweetness, her soothing encouragements and her obliging ways, softened untamed hearts and bestirred them to take up Christ's sweet yoke', moves to Ely to, once again, succeed her as abbess.

Meanwhile, Minster-in-Sheppey thrives on the site Seaxburh chose, high on an island surrounded on two sides by the River Swale, an offshoot of the Medway. With the broad Thames estuary to the north and the coast of Essex opposite and, to the south, the North Downs of Kent, there are wonderful views all around. This position puts Sheppey at the heart of transport links by water to London from the ports of Europe and by land into the centre of the Kingdom of

Kent. It's a very favourable place for trading and ministering to the faithful in the seventh and eighth centuries.

But its situation becomes the minster's undoing in the ninth when the Vikings come calling and see Sheppey as a great place to set up camp after a bit of pillaging and plundering. They destroy the minster but it's rebuilt only to be ransacked by Godwine, Earl of Wessex, and his kin in the eleventh century.

Breedon-on-the-Hill, Leicestershire

Breedon is on the edge of the lands belonging to the Tomsaetan people, ruled by their own council of ealdormen until the 650s when the Mercian king, Penda, extends his realm. Penda is the one remaining pagan king in England at the time but he allows Christian preaching and the conversion of those who are interested. Penda's eldest son, Peada, may or may not be Christian as sources differ, but his second son, Wulfhere [husband to Eormenhild mentioned above] rules from 658-675 and is definitely a Christian King of Mercia. He is followed as king by his younger brother, Aethelred, [675-704] who is also a Christian, and two of Penda's daughters are destined for sainthood.

But being a Christian doesn't stop Aethelred invading Kent at the start of his reign, ransacking the cathedral and priory in Rochester, reducing it to such a shambles that the bishop gives up and retires from office, rather than rebuild his see. In 704, it's Aethelred himself who retires, abdicating his throne to become a monk for the last twelve years of his life. Perhaps he hopes to make amends for his actions against the Church in Kent three decades before. Mercia, as the last bastion of pagan royalty, is no more but it takes far longer to convert fully the common folk of England.

In the minds of many churls, the old gods are still around. Every spring of fresh water, every marsh, hill top and outcrop of stone has a story to tell of the old ways. Neolithic henges, Bronze Age barrows and Iron Age hill forts are revered as the history markers of the Anglo-Saxons' adopted home. They see themselves as part of the landscape, continuing its ancient, unbroken history, and the acceptance of a new religion cannot entirely banish what the Christians regard as superstition. Make little offerings to appease the gods of streams and crossing points or of specific trees and, if you're a convert, say your prayers as well. This careful melding of beliefs will ensure both your physical and spiritual health and wellbeing.

For any of you male time-travellers who find the religious life appealing, you might enjoy a good home at the Minster of St Mary and St Hardulph at Breedon-on-the-Hill. Or if you're unwell – though you'll need to manage a long, steep climb – help can be found at Breedon. Way back, the site was an Iron Age hill fort with ditches and earthworks and within this well protected area, soon after 675, one of King Aethelred of Mercia's thegns – whom we only know by the Latinised version of his name, Friduricus – founds a minster with Hedda as its first abbot. It is possible the thegn was Fretheric, since the letter thorn [th] looks like a 'd' and there is a saint by this name listed as being buried here. St Hardulph, to whom the minster is dedicated, may be the king and saint Aerdulfus who is also noted as lying somewhere close by but no record of a king of that name survives. That doesn't mean he didn't exist as the survival of records is always a hit-and-miss affair.

Unfortunately, later quarrying has destroyed much of the graveyard with the bones of tall, well-built males and females being revealed, laid out in neat rows and dating to Anglo-Saxon times. This could suggest that Breedon is a double house but these mixed communities are usually overseen by an abbess, not an abbot. Who knows? But you can solve that mystery for us during your visit. Abbot Hedda makes sure Breedon gets noticed, encouraging endowments of land and making it very influential in the heartland of Mercia at a time when the Kings of Mercia are the most powerful and dominant in England. In 691, Hedda becomes Bishop of Lichfield, wielding even more influence.

Exterior view of St Mary's & St Hardulph's Church, Breedon-on-the-Hill, Leics.

However, Mercia goes into decline as the Danish Vikings become ever bolder. In 874, instead of raiding and then going home as they did previously, the Viking host over-winters at nearby Repton, which is definitely the site of a double house. They depose King Burghred of Mercia and, being pagan, loot minsters and force the monks and nuns to flee. But that isn't the end for Breedon because, by the late ninth century, the Danes themselves become Christian and the minster is re-founded by Bishop Aethelwold. During rebuilding, friezes and other exquisite stone carvings, dated c.800, are reused and can still be admired in the twenty-first century as lucky survivors. The Breedon Angel is a beautiful carving, said to be the earliest known angel figure in England. But who carved it?

Unlike the carved friezes and the remains of crosses, which show the intertwined birds and beasts so popular with Anglo-Saxon craftsmen, the angel and another figure carving in the south aisle are influenced by Eastern art, giving the Byzantine three-fingered sign of

Anglo-Saxon carving of a figure giving blessing in St Mary's & St Hardulph's Church, Breedon-on-the-Hill, Leics.

blessing – the index, middle and little fingers, representing the Father, Son and Holy Ghost, with the thumb holding down the ring finger.

Wareham, Dorset

There is one Anglo-Saxon kingdom we haven't heard much about so far, although this is soon to change – Wessex, the land of the West Saxons. Kent, Northumbria, Anglia and Mercia all have their day in the spot light, when their king is *Bretwalda*, or top dog, with the others serving as sub-kings, owing tributes and support in time of war to the over-king.

The kingdom of Wessex is centred along the fertile valley of the River Thames, stretching south to the coast, covering the modern counties of Devon, Dorset, Somerset, Wiltshire, Gloucestershire, Berkshire, Oxfordshire and Hampshire. King Cynegils who dies in AD643 is the first ruler of Wessex to be converted to Christianity – officially. I say 'officially' because you may notice how 'un-English' his name sounds, as do those of many of his predecessors: Cerdic, Cynric, Ceawlin, Coel, etc. and his successors: Cwichelm and Cenwalh. Despite Wessex calling itself a Saxon kingdom, the early kings have Brythonic names: the Celtic language of the Britons. If this means that the royal dynasty has origins among the Romano-Britons, it may also mean that they have remained Christians since Roman times, in name at least. Incidentally, this could also be evidence for the Anglo-Saxons not only living alongside the Celtic Britons who were already here but that the Britons hold on to authority in Wessex for a long while. Is there any clue to Celtic Christianity being practised in Wessex?

Wareham is a coastal town in modern Dorset, remodelled by King Aelfred in the ninth century as a burh or fortified township to protect the area from Viking raiders. It's laid out in a regular square with the thoroughfares forming a grid, just like a Roman town, defended on two sides by rivers with high walls and ramparts to the north and Poole harbour to the south. But Wareham is not a new town and predates Aelfred's time. In the south-east corner of the town is the Church of the Lady St Mary where King Beorhtric of Wessex lies buried, poisoned in 802 by his wife, a daughter of King Offa of Mercia. Apparently, evidence is growing that this is a minster long before Wessex becomes 'Christian' based on a Latin-speaking community of British clerics which serves a British population in Wareham. King Ine of Wessex [688-726] certainly passes a number of laws that make specific references to the *wergild* of his 'Welsh' subjects i.e., Britons, and details their ownership of property. This suggests that Wessex remains home to peoples other than the Anglo-Saxons and is possibly ruled by kings of British descent[2]. This means that Wareham had a minster, serving the community's spiritual needs and physical welfare very early on.

Chapter 7

Vikings

Who are the Vikings and are they always dangerous?

Defining the Vikings is as difficult as working out exactly who the Anglo-Saxons were when they first came here and their reasons for coming also vary. 'Viking' is a catch-all term for 'sea-warriors' or *saewicingas* whether they come from Norway, Sweden or Denmark – Scandinavians. *Wicengas* becomes 'Vikings'. So, these people are warriors and fighting men usually mean trouble but Scandinavians are not unknown in England before the raiding and pillaging begin when they come here to trade.

A monk from York, Alcuin, who left England to become the Emperor Charlemagne's priest and advisor, writes to his fellows back home in Northumbria after the first terrifying Viking raid on Lindisfarne in AD793. Alcuin bewails this pagan atrocity, despoiling the sacred abbey and resting place of St Cuthbert but then says it's the monks' and the peoples' own fault and serves them right. The reasons he gives are that the Christian locals are copying the heathen Scandinavian fashions, wearing 'luxurious dress', cutting their hair and trimming their beards like the Norwegians. How do the Northumbrians know about the raiders' grooming habits? And men set on pillaging and marauding aren't likely to be wearing their most opulent clothing. Clearly, they have met previously on friendlier terms.

Before they are branded as Vikings with a bad press, Scandinavians have been travelling vast distances across Eastern Europe, taking their shallow drafted boats along river systems and waterways as far as Byzantium [Constantinople or modern Istanbul], to the borders of the Islamic Empire, the Black Sea and the Eastern Mediterranean[1].

When rivers or lakes end, they carry the boats overland to the next waterway. They trade with Russians and Turks, acquiring silks and silver in exchange for furs and amber, items carved from walrus tusks and sealskin leather purses and shoes. No doubt, they trade with Christian Europe as well for grain, salt, linen and woollen textiles but this is where the problems begin. The Scandinavians are perfectly content with their pagan gods: Odin, Thor and the rest, but one man is determined to change all that.

Charlemagne – Charles the Great [r. 768-814] – King of the Franks and Holy Roman Emperor, sees it as his sacred task to convert these heathens to Christianity, whether they like it or not, at the point of a sword, if necessary. He is at war with the Saxons, i.e., the people still living in northern Germany and parts of southern Denmark, for thirty years. In 779, Widukind, the Saxon leader is defeated in battle and Charlemagne claims Saxony as part of his kingdom of Frankia. In 782, the Saxons rebel and Charlemagne forces 4,500 Saxon prisoners to convert to Christianity, to be baptised and then executed. Their pagan ideas of an afterlife are refuted so death must be terrifying, not knowing what to expect, being denied the rewards of joining their ancestors in the mead-hall of the gods.

Not content with mass murder, Charlemagne changes Saxony's culture by introducing draconian laws: rejecting baptism, eating meat during the Christian fasting period of Lent or cremating the dead according to pagan rites all become crimes punishable by death. Widukind finds sanctuary with his brother Sigfrid, King of Denmark, so the Danes know they are likely to be next on Charlemagne's list of heathen peoples to be forced to convert to Christianity. How can they possibly defend themselves against the mighty Frankish army which has conquered parts of Spain, Italy and southern France and already holds most of France, except for Brittany, and much of Germany as well?

Denmark does have a few assets in its favour, including the fact that King Sigfrid and his successor, Godfred, also rule the coastal areas of southern Norway and Sweden. Trading ventures have brought silver, making the elite few rich but coin is never enough to satisfy ambitious young warriors. Neither is the old-fashioned way of settling disputes over property and the narrow strips of coastal land by drawing lots, the losers being banished. Warriors expect to be rewarded for their prowess in battle with land and wealth and this isn't happening because the Danes are running out of both.

New horizons beckon and the Danes' biggest asset is crucial: technology. Their knowledge of shipbuilding is way ahead of everyone else's. Sleek, shallow-hulled longships powered by wind and sail, rather than manpowered by oars, are the most advanced vessels of the age[2]. Not only good for trade, these are sea-going war machines and young Scandinavians see the possibilities: if you can't inherit wealth and land, then you can take it – by force. The green and pleasant lands of England are just a few days sailing distance across the North Sea, if they're brave enough to venture out of sight of their home coastline, which these daring navigators are. So the peaceable traders you welcomed in the past now become the feared and terrible Vikings of the present.

To begin with, knowing that Charlemagne's worst has been carried out in the name of Christianity, the abbeys and minsters of coastal Eastern England and Scotland, rich and defenceless, are the most obvious prime targets. If you're a monk or a nun living anywhere near the coast, yes, Vikings are definitely dangerous and, as they grow more daring, living farther inland isn't a particularly safe alternative either.

Why do the invaders come to stay?

By AD850, Viking raids have become part of everyday life for many Anglo-Saxons, most summers seeing hit-and-run attacks which are almost impossible to prepare for with little chance of putting up a good defence. Viking ships are so swift that on a clear day you may have an hour's notice of a warband's arrival on your doorstep – just time enough, maybe, to bury your jewellery and coins. If it's misty or raining, there might be no warning at all until they come screaming and axe-wielding, rushing into your village, causing terror and chaos. And taking refuge in the church won't save you because that's likely to be their first target with its gold chalices, jewelled crosses and silver candlesticks. But at least you're safe in the winter when sea voyages are too dangerous, even for the daring Vikings.

That is until 851. That summer, the Vikings turn up to do their worst as usual. With a fleet of 350 ships, they attack the east coast of Kent, ransacking Canterbury before sailing up the River Thames to harry London, both of which had taken a beating previously in 842 with 'a great slaughter'. But when autumn comes, instead of sailing away, the Vikings stay, setting up camp for the winter on the Isle of Thanet where the Thames flows into the North Sea, having sacked the minster there. Green and fertile Kent supplies all their needs, unwillingly, in the hope that the enemy will restrain itself but Queen Seaxburh's Minster on the Isle of Sheppey is plundered and the Vikings camp close to its ruinous walls where the abbey's three wells provide fresh water. The Kentish people raise money – *danegeld* or, literally, 'gold for the Danes' – paying them to behave peaceably but the Vikings take the money and loot and pillage as they will anyway.

This is a sign of things to come. In 865, as the *Anglo-Saxon Chronicle* tells us, 'the Great Heathen Army' arrives to spend fifteen years subduing the kingdoms of Northumbria, Mercia and East Anglia. The Great Heathen Army is led by three brothers, sons of Ragnar Lothbrok, including Halfdan Ragnarsson, Ivar the Boneless and Ubba. They claim that this is payback for King Aella of Northumbria having slain their father, Ragnar, who had landed in the north of England with only two ships, bent on conquest. It hadn't ended well for the Danes on that occasion because Aella took Ragnar prisoner and, according to the sagas, flung him into a pit of snakes.

However, the brothers fare much better. They first land their army in East Anglia and King Edmund supplies them with horses, hoping they'll ride away and pillage somewhere else, which they do, but they return to their landing site at Thetford in Suffolk to spend the winter.

🖈 Top Tip

England's only venomous snake is the adder or viper. Its bite hurts like a bee sting but isn't fatal to humans so being in a pit of snakes wouldn't be pleasant but Ragnar probably died of lack of water rather than snake bite. But that's not such great saga material.

In 866, Halfdan and Ivar lead an attack on York, Aella's capital. They choose 1 November, the important feast day of All Saints when most people are at prayer in York Minster, using their religious practices against the Christians. The plan goes brilliantly as the Vikings capture the town, and re-found it as a Danish settlement: Jorvik, with a puppet king of their choice.

Their target for the campaigning season of 867 is the kingdom of Mercia. Despite having military assistance from King Aethelred I of Wessex, the Vikings force the Mercians to come to terms, including the payment of more *danegeld,* and then overwinter in Nottingham. It seems the invaders can go wherever they please: back to York for the winter of 868-69, followed by a return to East Anglia in 869 where young Aelfred of Wessex [not yet a king] joins King Edmund in an attempt to defeat Halfdan and Ivar.

Unfortunately, King Edmund is captured by the Vikings who demand that he renounces his Christian faith and shares his throne with their leaders. When he refuses, he is tied to a tree, shot full of arrows before being decapitated. The story goes that a talking wolf guards Edmund's severed head, calling out 'Hic, hic, hic!' [Latin for 'Here, here, here!] to alert the king's followers so that the martyr's body parts can be reunited. Where he is slain is uncertain but his burial place still bears his name – Bury St Edmunds, in Suffolk.

The Vikings or Danes now rule half of England, from York to Essex lying north of the River Thames with footholds in Kent which is now part of Wessex. England seems doomed to be conquered and who can prevent it?

Mural of St Edmund in St Peter & St Paul's Church, Pickering, Yorks.

Did You Know?

England celebrates St George as its patron saint on 23 April, flying his flag of a red cross on a white background but George isn't England's first patron saint. Petitions have been made to Parliament to have St Edmund reinstated to this position as he was before Richard the Lionheart visited St George's tomb in the Holy Land while on crusade in the twelfth century. In which case we should fly the flag of the White Dragon on a red back ground on 20 November: the date of Edmund's murder.

Aelfred, King of Wessex

The year is 870 and the Vikings are joined by reinforcements from home. A 'Great Summer Army' arrives from Scandinavia, led by Bacseg, and this huge combined force has Wessex as its objective, spending the winter at Reading, a royal estate situated between the Thames and a tributary, the River Kennet. The Vikings build a long earthwork embankment between the two rivers but the campaigning season is about to begin early in the New Year. While many Vikings are busy with the construction work, others go about plundering the local countryside for supplies. At Englefield, six miles to the west, the pillagers meet opposition when Aethelwulf, Ealdorman of Berkshire, brings a force to fight them. The Vikings' leader is killed, along with many of his men, and the rest scurry back to Reading. There, those who have remained behind 'fight like wolves', fatally injuring the plucky ealdorman.

Four days later, on 8 January 871, the Vikings and the West Saxon army, known as the *fürd,* face each other again at Ashdown on the Berkshire Downs, though the site has never been identified for certain, so maybe you can solve this mystery for us. The West Saxons are led by King Aethelred I, ably assisted by his younger brother Aclfred; the Vikings by King Bacseg and his jarls. It's a bloody clash indeed. Bacseg and at least five of his leading jarls die in the fray but if Aethelred thinks Wessex is victorious, his triumph doesn't last long because 871 becomes known as 'the year of nine engagements', i.e. battles.

Two weeks later, the Viking host win the day at Basing, Hampshire [now Old Basing], driving the West Saxons from the field. They fight it out again two months later at Meretun – a place not yet identified – but the outcome is indecisive. However, it seems King Aethelred may be seriously wounded in the fray because he dies a few weeks later at Easter. His sons are youngsters and the Witan or royal council decide that twenty-one-year-old Aelfred, proven in battle, is to be king. The Anglo-Saxons don't hold with the later Norman idea that the eldest son always inherits, rather the most suitable candidate, usually a royal relative, is chosen for the task. But whoever is in charge, the fight against the invaders must continue. A month on and another indecisive battle is fought at Wilton in Wiltshire, heartland of Wessex. Things are getting desperate for the Anglo-Saxons.

The following winter, the Great Heathen Army is encamped at Lundenwic, on the edge of Mercian territory, insulting Aelfred and Wessex from their very own doorstep and a payment of *danegeld* is intended to ensure the Danes behave. It's a huge relief then when a rebellion in Northumbria against the puppet king set up by the Vikings drags the Danish army north to sort out the problem. They spend the winter of 872-73 in the sub-kingdom of Lindsey [now part of Lincolnshire] and the Mercians pay *danegeld* once again, hoping to keep the peace. As winter comes around again, the Vikings choose Repton on the River Trent in Derbyshire for their quarters, creating a semi-permanent base from which to attack the surrounding Mercian lands and desecrating the double monastery of St Wystan there. This time, Burghred, King of Mercia, and his wife, Aethelswith, Aelfred's sister, are forced to flee all the way to Rome, never to return. As they did before in Northumbria, the Vikings set up a puppet regime with Ceolwulf II, described at the time as 'a foolish thegn', as King of Mercia, in name only, so long as he co-operates with his new masters.

Mercian kings are buried at Repton so occupying this place is quite a political statement: 'We Vikings are in charge!' A beautiful cross is broken and thrown into the defensive ditch. What is more the Vikings use this Christian site to bury their own dead by pagan rites, undermining the Anglo-Saxons' beliefs and any hopes they have that their God will protect them.

A long-term camp like this gives them the chance to repair weapons and make good their ships – thousands of iron ship nails have been found here – where, in the ninth century, the Trent flows close by with a place to beach their craft. Clothes and shoes need mending and the local produce which fed the monks and nuns now fills Viking bellies.

During twentieth-century archaeological excavations, a number of graves were found and Grave 511 was special. Buried as close as possible to where Mercian kings were interred without actually being inside the ruins of the church, the occupant, male, was buried like those in neighbouring graves, with weapons – a sword and knife – as well as a silver Thor's hammer pendant. Forensic pathology showed

The Anglo-Saxon crypt of St Wystan's Church, Repton, Derbys.

that he suffered a traumatic death, receiving a blow to the head which knocked him down, evidence suggesting he was wearing a helmet at the time. Then, as he lay on the ground, an axe sliced through his femur at the hip, severing the femoral artery. He would have bled to death in a few minutes. It's also likely that the cut took away his manhood and a thoughtful mourner had supplied the warrior's lack in the afterlife by placing a boar's tusk at his groin with the humerus [wing bone] of a jackdaw, possibly to symbolise Odin's pet ravens, for good measure. After death, evidence shows his internal organs were removed.

But G511 had a companion in death, interred separately but with both graves covered by the same rectangular stone of fine Anglo-Saxon workmanship. This was G295, a younger man who had suffered horrific injuries, buried somewhat later than the warrior and with only a knife. More recently, detailed DNA and isotope analysis has told their likely story: tall, blue-eyed, fair-haired, Danish Vikings, father and son, the elder probably balding. But who were they? Cat Jarman's research has unearthed their possible identities and, if correct, shows the Vikings at their worst and best[3].

Olaf, a Viking king, ruled Dublin in Ireland in the 850s and 860s. The *Annals of Ulster* tell of his actions throughout the British Isles,

The sword of a Viking buried at Repton in Mercia, now in Derby Museum.

often raiding and pillaging alongside his brother, Ivar the Boneless. If this is true, Olaf was yet another son of the semi-mythical Ragnar Lothbrok and brother to Halfdan and the others. Olaf was killed in 874, fighting in Scotland against Constantin, King of the Picts. He would've been aged around forty – which fits the findings for G511. It's possible that Ivar or Halfdan had their brother's body eviscerated so it wouldn't decompose too swiftly and brought it 'home' to their winter quarters at Repton for burial with full Viking rites, showing them at their best as loving brothers.

Not so the burial of G295. Olaf had a son and heir, Eysteinn and the *Annals of Ulster* relate that in the following year 875, Olaf's son was 'deceitfully killed by Halfdan' who, if the stories are true, was his uncle. So, this was no glorious warrior's death in battle, ensuring Eysteinn a place in Valhalla at his father's side; this was the Vikings at their worst, committing cold blooded murder on a young relative. And we can guess Halfdan's motive because, in due course, he will become King of Dublin, setting up a permanent Viking settlement there in Ireland and getting Eysteinn out of the way removes the closest competition for the post.

But back to what is known for certain. The Vikings are now so powerful, their army so huge, they can afford to divide their forces. Halfdan goes north, wintering in 874-75 beside the River Tyne and, during the following campaign season, plunders over the border, into Scotland, fighting the Picts and Britons of Strathclyde. This Viking horde is unstoppable. However, in 876, Halfdan brings his men back south, into Northumbria and his tactics change in a surprising way. Having had enough of ravaging and pillaging for all they need to survive, Halfdan shares out the conquered land between his men and 'they begin to plough and support themselves', as the *Anglo-Saxon Chronicle* tells us. Nobody plants crops which must be tended, weeded and harvested months later unless they plan to stay around to benefit from the results, so now we know: the Vikings aren't intending to go home to Scandinavia any time soon. What is more, these occupied territories are under Danish, not English, jurisdiction – the area that becomes recognised as the Danelaw.

Despair and compromise

The other portion of the Great Army has its eyes on wealthy, fertile Wessex and they aren't going to miss out on this jewel in England's crown if they get the chance. In 874, Guthrum, leader of this second army, rides from Cambridge in Mercian territory, avoiding any entanglements with Aelfred, straight across Wessex, all the way to Wareham in Dorset on the south coast. From there, the Danes raid as and when they please and although they agree a truce with Aelfred, they sneak off under cover of darkness and set themselves up in Exeter in Devon which still has its old Roman walls in a defensible condition.

Aelfred rides in pursuit with his small force but battle has to be avoided. They exchange oaths and both sides give over hostages as a guarantee that they'll keep their side of the deal. Guthrum, who'd had the upper hand until now, has recently lost in a storm, 120 of his supporting longships which kept pace with his army, sailing along the south coast. With his numbers depleted, Guthrum agrees to Aelfred's terms and withdraws back into Mercia, to Gloucester, another town with Roman defences.

But if Aelfred breathes a sigh of relief as Guthrum is busy, arranging to rule eastern Mercia while Ceolwulf 'reigns' over the western lands towards Wales, it's premature. Winter isn't usually the season for campaigning, especially the period of celebration for the Anglo-Saxons from Christmas to Twelfth Night. The Vikings are pagan but they know the Christian calendar well enough to realise that Aelfred and Wessex will be thinking about praying, feasting and making merry – probably not in that order – rather than preparing for war. In 877-78, Guthrum is based in Gloucester once more and, having given his Christian adversaries twelve days to drink themselves into a state of total unpreparedness, if not oblivion, he and his men ride across the frozen Wessex countryside. They attack the royal estate at Chippenham in Wiltshire, one of Aelfred's most important residences, on 6 January 878. Choosing a Church feast day is a common pagan ploy but fighting in January when you may have to battle bad weather and the cold as well is unexpected. It may be that Guthrum hopes to catch Aelfred himself at Chippenham, feet up before a good fire, mead cup in hand, and by taking him prisoner or killing him the Vikings' victory will be swift and complete. But Aelfred isn't there.

However, Chippenham itself is worth having with its granaries and barns full, larders stocked and mead jugs brimming. You can imagine Guthrum taking his ease in royal splendour in the well-defended Anglo-Saxon hall he has taken with only a few royal officials and the local peasants to oppose him. Now he has an excellent base inside Wessex from which to hunt down the king and acquire his kingdom – the last in England to resist the Vikings. As the *Anglo-Saxon Chronicle* tells us: 'the Danes rode over the land of Wessex'. Hampshire folk flee across the Solent to the Isle of Wight; Ealdorman Wulfhere, the king's chief man in Wiltshire 'deserts his king and country' and goes abroad. Aelfred's private estates are mostly in Dorset but the *Chronicle* says nothing of the county putting up a fight. Since the *Chronicle* is written at the king's instigation, its silence maybe damning. Perhaps Dorset surrenders to the Danes, believing that submission is inevitable either sooner or later. Devon doesn't warrant a mention.

Aelfred and his few remaining warriors are reduced to making hit-and-run attacks on the Danes: more of an irritation to the invaders than a serious threat, hiding out in woodland and marsh. The only ray of light in this dismal predicament shines in Somerset and it's a feeble glow: Ealdorman Aethelnoth of Somerset has a small, loyal force lurking in the forest near the royal estate of Somerton, covering the possibility of a Danish advance along the Roman Foss Way, though how his little band might prevent the Viking army from marching onward is hard to see. This is Aelfred's most desperate hour; he and his men going hungry in the marshlands which a rainstorm can transform from a swamp to a lake in a couple of hours. It's been six weeks since they last had dry feet but I catch up with Aelfred in a swineherd's cottage on the Isle of Athelney where the damp, dishevelled king is trying to dry out:

'My Lord Aelfred…'

'Shush. People here don't know me and Guthrum mustn't learn of my whereabouts. Who are you?'

'A loyal well-wisher,'

'You'd better be. One wrong word and I'll slay you myself.'

'Understandable. How does it feel to be a lost cause?'

'How dare you! Mine is not a lost cause. Why, just a few days ago, I received Divine inspiration in a dream.'

'Really? Tell me.'

'Aye, well…' [Aelfred coughs]. 'This dampness gets into your chest. Bald, my leech, says I must keep warm and dry because of my delicate health. Not much chance of that, is there?'

'No. I've got a sniffle myself.'

'Keep it to yourself, churl. Bad enough that I must bide with a pig-keeper without sharing your foul airs.'

'I'm not the swineherd.'

'Oh. Never mind who you are. See those barley loaves on the griddle? I'm to make certain they don't scorch while the wife is outside, plucking a curlew for my dinner. You watch the bread and I'll tell you about my Divine dream.'

'Great. I love a story.'

'Listen! There we were, me and my few good men, up to our armpits in mud, slithering like eels through the reeds, trying to catch anything with a bit of meat on it for dinner. Four days since our last meal… a clutch of moorhen's eggs. At last, Wulfrid almost fell upon a mallard on her nest with chicks, sitting out the downpour. We found higher ground where an ash tree grew. As you know, ash wood burns when wet and Outred is a genius with flint and striker. Anyway… he got a fire going while the rest of us plucked feathers. Aye, an Aetheling of noble heritage, I am indeed, but I can do common tasks as required. Are you shocked?'

'Not really.'

'You should be. Now where was I? Oh, aye, Outred cooked our birds. We were giving thanks unto God for our frugal meal – hardly a mouthful each – before tucking into it when a stranger arrives. Straight out of the mist he comes, claiming he's a pilgrim… a hungry one. Of course, the others weren't eager to share but I know you can't be too careful with holy men, even dubious-looking pilgrims. So we shared and, I tell you, the pilgrim ate most of it. Then he said he had to leave, sorry if we were still hungry but if we went fishing at dawn we would be well fed. And he was gone. In the morning, my men took their boots off, dipped them into the water – they were soaking anyway – and out they came: full of fish, so the pilgrim was right. We had a huge breakfast and enough left for supper as well.'

'What about your dream?'

'I'm coming to that. Don't rush a good story-teller. And have a look at those barley loaf-cake things.'

'They're doing nicely. Nearly done.'

'So… last night, here, in this flea-bitten hovel, I had a dream. St Cuthbert himself appeared to me and I recognised him as the pilgrim we fed the other day. Do you know what he said?'

'What?'

'He said, "Aelfred" – he knew my name – "Stay strong and courageous and your descendants will be Kings of England and rule all Albion!" That's what he told me.'

'And you believe him?'

'He's a saint. He foretold our fine catch of fish. He's my Divine inspiration and I'll never give up now.' [Sniffs] 'What's burning? You foolish churl! You've burnt the cakes and I'll get the blame, won't I?'

'I'm afraid so, Aelfred.'[4]

🔖 Top Tip

The story of Aelfred burning the 'cakes' is legendary and you may be surprised that the Vikings have a similar tale about one of their heroes, the marvellously named Ragnar Hairybreeks or 'hairy pants'. He burned a batch of loaves/cakes too. So whichever side you find you're sharing a fireside with on a dark evening, Anglo-Saxon or Dane, this is a tale you can tell to please everyone and storytellers usually get a free meal and drink – worth remembering.

The decisive battle and aftermath

As the weather improves, in May 878, Aelfred sends out messengers, summoning the remaining ealdormen and thegns on whom he can still rely to meet him at Ecgberht's Stone, on the border between the three counties of Dorset, Somerset and Wiltshire, probably a traditional muster point. Asser, who later writes Aelfred's biography, records how, when the Wessex army gathers and sees the king, alive and well after a long winter of silence, 'they receive him as if restored to life … they are filled with immense joy'. Aelfred himself must be equally delighted and relieved to discover he has command of a force large enough to take on Guthrum and his Danish host.

The following day, Aelfred leads his men north-east, about twelve miles to Iley Oak, another recognised meeting place. Here they make camp on high ground, overlooking the flood plain of the River Wylye, and if the weather is clear, they can see Chippenham, the enemy base camp, sixteen miles away across open country. No one knows whether both sides have scouts and spies on the look-out or whether messages are exchanged, inviting the other to do battle but the two sides meet at Ethandune [Edington]. Edington Hill is six miles from Iley Oak, on the edge of Salisbury Plain, the ideal terrain for military manoeuvres even in the twenty-first century. It's perfect for the Anglo-Saxons' shield wall tactics. The only account we have of this history-changing encounter is Asser's and he's not much of a war correspondent, unfortunately. He tells us that Aelfred 'fights fiercely with a compact shield wall' but 'fighting with' is ambiguous – does it refer to his Wessex compatriots at his side or the Danish opposition? Asser says: 'And one day later [Aelfred went] to Edington and there he fought against the entire Host and put it to flight and afterward pursued it up to the fortification'. That's his entire account. All we know for certain is that Wessex won the day. We're not even sure to which 'fortification' Aelfred chased the fleeing Danes – maybe all the way back to Chippenham but more likely to Bratton Camp, an Iron Age hillfort just over a mile away.

It's also possible that Aelfred wasn't so alone as Asser describes because, soon after, coins are minted by Aelfred and Ceolwulf, puppet king of western Mercia, as joint kings. These may be issued to celebrate a joint triumph over the Danes but Ceolwulf dies soon after – of battle injuries? – and is written out of the tale.

Whether Mercians fought alongside or not, the West Saxons lay siege to the Danes for a fortnight, wearing them down with 'fear, cold and hunger'. This suggests Guthrum isn't at well-supplied Chippenham but holed up in a temporary fortress like Bratton. Not sure that cold weather would be a problem in May the Danes surrender and give hostages to Aelfred to guarantee their good behaviour. The defeated Vikings are ordered to leave Wessex for good, along with the sub-kingdoms of Kent and Sussex. Guthrum has to submit to baptism as a Christian and accept Aelfred, not only as his godfather, but as his overlord. It's also agreed that the Danes should live beyond the imagined boundary of the Danelaw, with Anglo-Saxon territory to the south and west and the Vikings to the north and east with York or Jorvik as their capital. There, they take up crafts like knitting, weaving and metal-working, trading with their Anglo-Saxon neighbours and farming the land. They even re-introduce the novelty of bathing, forgotten since the Romans left long ago.

Meanwhile, not quite trusting his long-standing enemies, Aelfred realises the necessity of a navy, to combat the Vikings before they set foot on land. He also reorganises the army, the *furd,* and sets up the burh system of fortified towns, often re-using old Roman towns and rebuilding their defensive walls.

Lundenwic, as you may recall, lies to the west of what was once Roman Londinium, a busy trading post but entirely undefended. Now Aelfred uses the opportunity to move Lundenwic within the remaining Roman walls of the abandoned city. The walls need repair before they can be reckoned a reasonable defensive barrier but at least the foundations are a good start. The Anglo-Saxons call their defended towns 'burhs' so the place gets a new name – Lundenburh – as well as a suitable residence for a king, thought to be to the north of St Paul's Cathedral, although no definite archaeological evidence of it has yet been found.

Perhaps, you may be fortunate enough to live in Aelfred's mead-hall or at least have the chance to take it easy for a while now the Danish problem is pretty much sorted out. Take the opportunity to admire the finer things in life, to indulge in leisure activities, as we'll see in the next chapter.

Chapter 8

Arts, Crafts and Literature

One thing at which the Anglo-Saxons excel is storytelling, whether long, heroic sagas like *Beowulf* or 'origin' tales that set the people into the British landscape to provide them with a history in their adopted homeland. After dark, by the fire in the mead-hall as the flames die down, the *scop* or storyteller keeps the audience enthralled, providing incidental music, strumming his lyre, building tension or lulling his listeners into a false sense of relief.

Prehistoric sites, such as henges and barrows, are given new stories to make them relevant. For example, Grimes Graves is the name the Anglo-Saxons give to the Neolithic flint mines still visible in the twenty-first century near Thetford in Suffolk, Grim being another persona of the god Woden.

A myth is created to explain Stonehenge that it marks the burial place of the Britons slain in battle by Hengist sometime after the Anglo-Saxons first arrived. The stones were brought here by a magician, possibly Merlin, from either Ireland or maybe Africa – versions differ[2]. The point is to give the Anglo-Saxons a sense of belonging to their new home, grounding them in the ancient landscape.

There are probably hundreds, perhaps thousands, of different tales to choose from but, of course, in the early years, before Christianity takes hold, the Anglo-Saxons are an oral society and don't put these stories in writing. What a huge loss that is to us who come after. Once the new religion is established, legends involving Woden, Thunor and the old gods are no longer suitable subjects and their stories are cast aside. Only one has survived: a pagan tale of heroes and monsters long remembered and finally put to parchment with Christian overtones to make it more acceptable. The King of the

A reproduction of the Anglo-Saxon 'Trossingen' lyre.[1]

Geats in the story, Hygelac, died c.520 and the oral elements are of the sixth century; the Old English style is that of early eighth-century Northumbria and the lone surviving manuscript dates to c.1000. This is the epic poem *Beowulf.*

Of men and monsters

Beowulf is set in the ancestral Scandinavian homelands of the Anglo-Saxons, involving the Scyldings or Danes – the victims of the piece, so this story appeals to the Vikings as well – and the adventurous Geats, a tribe in southern Sweden. Their King Hygelac is real enough, killed doing battle with the Franks, but if the heroic Beowulf ever existed, his history lives on only in this legend.

Hrothgar, King of the Danes, has built a fabulous mead-hall to celebrate his successes, 'The Hall of the Stag', or *Heorot*. But Hrothgar and his warriors can't enjoy their mead in peace because a monster lurks outside in the darkness, one who loathes the sounds of merrymaking inside the hall. This is Grendal, flesh-ripper, bone-gnasher, who breaks into the hall, carrying thirty thegns away to his lair where he lives with his mother. This horror is repeated, night after night, as Grendel commits every outrage and slaughter imaginable and the Danes dare not sleep. They pray to their gods – 'the Lord God was unknown to them', the Christian scribe points out – and nobody can devise a plan to defeat the monster. But news of the situation travels across the sea to the Geats and Prince Beowulf – sea-skilled in his seaworthy wave-cutter – sails with fourteen men, over the swan's riding, to help the beleaguered Danes.

Beowulf and his men, arrayed for war in ring-mail, their helmets sparkling with glancing boar emblems and brilliant with gold, have to convince the Danish guardian of their good intentions before they can meet King Hrothgar. Then, after much discussion during which the Geats explain their credentials and Beowulf does a lot of boasting – 'I have bound five giants… crushed sea-serpents by night… shall I not try a single match against this fiend Grendel?' – it's agreed that the king and his thegns will sleep elsewhere, leaving the Geats in the hall to await the monster's nightly visit. Beowulf declares that he'll fight Grendal but not with weapons because the monster knows nothing of arms and this must be a fair fight. Rather, the Christian God will decide who wins the contest. Not surprisingly, his men reckon they won't live to go home.

Grendel arrives and grabs the nearest Geat, bolting gobbets of flesh and sucking his veins dry, but then he meets Beowulf and realises he's never encountered a man with a stronger grip on middle earth's acres. He tries to run but our hero holds him fast. They fight hard, the hall barely surviving their efforts, Grendel screaming in pain. At last, the monster breaks free but his arm is torn off, 'a rip in the giant flesh-frame showing', and he stumbles away, death sick, home to his mother to die in his lair. The Geats sleep peacefully. All is well. Is this the 'happy ever after' ending? Of course not. Grendel's mother, the black-hearted, gluttonous ogress, wants vengeance for her son.

And so, the epic adventure continues, probably told nightly, episode by episode, like a soap opera. Beowulf destroys Grendel's mother, although she's far more difficult to kill, then he becomes a right and goodly king, a renowned ring-bestower, before having to slay a dragon in his old age and being mortally wounded. His body is cremated on a huge pyre, the ashes interred with his jewels and weapons and a great mound raised over the tomb. This is definitely a pagan burial despite the scribe adding that 'Heaven swallowed his smoke'[3].

If you're a *scop* you may embellish and 'improve' the story however you think will please the audience. The Anglo-Saxons are brilliant at inventing synonyms such as 'bone house' and 'flesh frame' for body; 'swan riding' and 'whale way' for the sea. How many ways can you describe the sun? In a poem called 'The Phoenix', taken from a collection of Anglo-Saxon literature known as *The Exeter Book* – more on this below – the anonymous poet writes:

[The phoenix] beholds the journey of the sun
And comes to meet God's candle,
Eagerly watches the jewel of gladness
When that noblest of stars rises up
Above the waves, gleaming from the east;
The Father's ancient work glimmers with ornaments,
Bright token of God.[4]

Here, the poet makes full use of what the Anglo-Saxons term the 'word-hoard' – their mental thesaurus or treasury of words – giving five different names to the sun in just seven lines. A marvellous piece of invention, isn't it? Make up your own descriptions, the more colourful and alliterative as possible, and you'll certainly be invited back to entertain in the mead-hall. Learning to play the lyre to accompany your stories, told in this rich-sounding language with its rolling Rs, will be a bonus.

Gorgeous gold and fabulous finds

One of the most spectacular Anglo-Saxon finds made in England was the Sutton Hoo ship burial excavated in Suffolk in 1939. The marvellous array of jewellery and other artefacts buried with the ship proved that the description of Beowulf's funerary goods is based in fact. It's thought to be the final resting place of Raedwald, King of East Anglia, who ruled from 599 and died in 624 or 625. No physical bodily remains were found so, perhaps like Beowulf, he was cremated first and his ashes buried inside the ship before it was covered with a great mound of sandy earth. Or maybe the body had simply disappeared into the soil, a high level of phosphates being all that remained of either ashes or bones. But the splendid grave goods, the fact that a fine ship was given over to the deceased and the trouble that was taken with the burial all indicate that a VIP was interred here, overlooking his domains.

Of Raedwald's precious objects, some are of the most exquisite metalwork – the most famous being the incredible helmet, constructed of iron overlaid with bronze foil with bronze strips, clips and nails holding it together and lined with padded leather for comfort. The king would be well protected by ear-flaps, neck guard, eyebrow, nose and cheek-pieces. It is most probably made in England although it has elements of Roman traditional parade headgear and hints at Scandinavian style decoration – a glorious testament to the Anglo-Saxon smith.

A reconstruction of the Sutton Hoo helmet.

Every warrior requires a shield and Raedwald's is circular, over three feet across [90cms +], made of lime wood covered with leather and rimmed with gilt-bronze. It's decorated with gilded birds of prey and an intricate dragon with a huge gilded boss in the centre – a weapon in itself. It's thought the shield is for show, rather than use in battle, and may be made by Swedish craftsmen working in England. The king is also provided with six spears of different types, one laid by his sword, ready for immediate use, along with three angons [javelins meant to be thrown], an axe-hammer and a mailcoat. Raedwald also has a top-of-the-range sword, as you'd expect, in a fabulous scabbard and an exquisite belt to hang it from. The sword has a pattern-welded blade forged from iron rods, twisted and hammered to create a herringbone design within the blade. This is the blade-smith's craft at its ultimate best so the decoration has to be of the same standard. The goldsmith has worked his/her magic on both the leather, wool-lined scabbard and the sword hilt with gold work inlaid with cloisonné garnets; the stones matched for colour from pinkish red to purple. A cloak with shoulder clasps of gold and garnets completes the warrior's ensemble. Raedwald was fully arrayed for war in the next life as well as proclaiming his incredible wealth and the power of kingship.

A Sutton Hoo cloisonné shoulder clasp.

Other grave goods include silverware from the Mediterranean: dishes, bowls and spoons – two of the last with a Christian connection, though whether this suggests the king has leanings towards the new religion or if they are simply traded objects we cannot say. After all, this is definitely a pagan burial but Raedwald could be hedging his bets in the afterlife. Drinking horns, a set of wooden cups, three marvellous 'hanging bowls' of bronze with British Celtic motifs of millefiori glass, buckets, flagons and cauldrons, including a huge bronze one which can hold almost 100 litres, provide for the feasting. A maplewood, six-stringed lyre is ready to be played to entertain the king in quieter moments as well as gaming pieces and dice. A purse with an inlaid lid of bone or ivory contains 37 gold coins of Gaulish minting, dated 575-625, to pay the king's way to the next world and, to make certain the gods are aware of Raedwald's elevated rank, he has a whetstone 'sceptre' surmounted with a small bronze stag. Nothing comparable has been found anywhere else. You may think such magnificence as found at Sutton Hoo must be an exceptional case but there is another not so far away in Essex.

Southend-on-Sea in Essex is a modern seaside resort, famous for the longest pier in the world, but in Anglo-Saxon times it is simply the 'south-end' of the now-little-known village and royal residence of Prittlewell on the north bank of the Thames estuary. In 2003, a burial of royal magnificence was discovered. Among the grave goods are some gold-foil crosses placed over the eyes of the deceased – of whom nothing remains but a few teeth fragments – suggesting Christian influence. Saeberht, King of Essex, who converted to Christianity at the insistence of his uncle, Aethelberht, King of Kent, seems a likely candidate at first. He died in 616 and was said to have wanted to be buried at Westminster. Or could it be his Christian grandson, Sigeberht the Good? We know it can't be any of Saeberht's sons as they are devotees of the old gods. Carbon dating of a drinking horn and a wooden cup to 575-605 make it too early for Saeberht or his grandson so it's more likely to be that of Saeberht's brother, Seaxa, who died in c.605. However, if the horn and cup are old heirlooms, the carbon dating may be irrelevant. Perhaps you can make enquiries and solve the mystery for us.

The corpse lies in a wooden coffin, well dressed with a solid gold belt buckle. His face is covered by a cloth trimmed with gold braid. The grave goods are arranged separately around the chamber, not with the body, perhaps a nod to the Christian influence of burial without equipment for the afterlife. Nevertheless, the deceased is provided with a fine pattern-welded sword with an ivory hilt decorated with gold wire which is still bright today, placed in a wood, leather and sheep's wool scabbard. The wool lining keeps the blade greased and shiny.

A maplewood box, painted with red and yellow ochre and white gypsum pigments is a unique find. It holds the man's personal items – a silver spoon, a knife in a scabbard, fire-lighting equipment, possibly an item of underwear and a cylindrical box which may hold a Christian relic or a good luck charm. Gold coins of Gaulish minting – like Raedwald's – are dated no earlier than 580. A folding iron stool is another unique item and may be a *gif-stol* from which the lord would give judgement and, as the name suggests, reward and give gifts to his men. A copper alloy Syrian flagon, hanging bowls, a maplewood lyre with garnet decoration, the stones originating in Sri Lanka, are other fine artefacts along with some costly textiles but the best are the coloured glass pots, exquisite and so delicate, it's a wonder they survive.

The glassware was made in Kent on the opposite bank of the Thames estuary and these at Prittlewell aren't the only examples in Essex. A very similar blue glass pot was found in another high status burial at nearby Broomfield. The buckles for the lord's garters and the metal coffin fittings are all of Kentish design and manufacture so obviously there are close connection to Aethelberht's kingdom across the river.

But not every beautiful example of the Anglo-Saxons' goldsmiths' work is buried with the dead. The Alfred Jewel was unearthed during ploughing in 1693 in Somerset, not far from Athelney where Alfred took refuge between his battles with Guthrum and the Danish Great

Exquisite Prittlewell glassware made in Kent.

Army. The jewel is part of an 'aestel', a pointer to help readers to follow lines of text without putting grubby fingers on the page. It consists of a cloisonné enamel image of a figure in a teardrop shape, protected by a thin layer of clear rock crystal and surrounded by the finest gold work inscribed with the words AELFRED MEC HEHT GEWYRCAN – 'Aelfred ordered me to be made'. The jewel tapers to a dragon head at the base, its open mouth forming the socket in which the pointer, probably made of ivory, was once riveted.

Once Aelfred is settled in his kingdom, having pushed the Danes back within the limits of the Danelaw, he is determined to improve the standard of education of his subjects. To this end, he learns Latin, having learned to read English as a child, and commissions translations of various religious texts from Latin. As Aelfred tells us:

> *When I remember how the knowledge of Latin had formerly decayed throughout England and yet many could read English writing, I began, amongst other various*

and manifold troubles of this kingdom, to translate into English… sometimes word by word and sometimes according to sense…

The king sets up the writing of the *Anglo-Saxon Chronicle* which continues to be kept up to date in various texts until the death of King Stephen in 1154, telling the history of the people of Wessex and then of England. Some of the early entries are very brief, to the effect: 'In 671 Cenwalh passed away and Seaxburh his queen reigned one year after him'. But this is all that's required to remind the Anglo-Saxon storyteller with a prodigious memory of a lengthy epic to enthral his/her audience in the mead-hall. When Aelfred distributes these manuscripts across his lands, he includes an aestal to assist reading and the jewel is believed to be one of these gifts.

Whoever crafted the jewel was incredibly skilled and we have a second piece of his/her workmanship in the Minster Lovell Jewel. This is a circular aestal with a geometrical floral design of blue, green and white cloisonné enamel, surrounded by gold work in the shape of petals and faced with rock crystal just like the Alfred Jewel although the socket is fairly plain. It's so similar that experts agree both are made by the same hand. Found by the roadside near Minster Lovell, Oxfordshire, in 1872, it is kept with its royal cousin at the Ashmolean Museum in Oxford.

These gorgeous objects seem to have been lost accidentally but other precious artefacts are buried intentionally, as is the case with the incredible Staffordshire hoard, uncovered by

Alfred's jewel, the handle of an aestal or pointer for reading text.

metal-detectorists in 2009. In the twenty-first century, we don't know why around 700 gold and silver items, most broken into thousands of pieces, were hidden in a pit, never to be retrieved by whoever buried them. Let's ask the man with the spade:

'Hey! Churl! What are doing? Why are smashing that superb helmet, you dolt? That's worthy of a king, that is.'

'What this? Spoils of war. I collected most of this myself from one battle or another and got the scars to prove it. See? [He pulls up his sleeve to show me a half-healed scar. Nasty.]

'Whose man are you?'

'King Penda's of Mercia. You heard of him?'

'Aye. He's a great warrior.'

'He's a great, greedy troll; that's what he is and if he knows I've got all this treasure gathering, he'll want it for himself. Well, he's not getting his claws on it. It's mine… all of it.'

'Show me what you have before you bury it.'

'Why?'

'Because I'm an archaeologist.'

'A what?'

'Never mind. Because I'm interested. What are those? They're exquisite.'

'Decorations from sword hilts mostly. Valuable. When I get the chance, I'll come back, dig up a few bits at a time, melt them down or barter them for something useful. If I do it all at once, it'll look suspicious, won't it? Penda might learn of my hoard. I'm not stupid you know.'

'Why have you broken everything? Surely, a whole sword is worth more? And the helmet is useless now.'

'I don't want anyone recognising their own sword, if I tried to sell it, do I now? Besides, it's easier to bury it in bits.'

'Those aren't sword decorations. That looks like a cross.'

'Aye, well if those Christian priests are foolish enough to think wearing a cross will protect them, instead of carrying a shield, then it serves them right.'

'You killed a priest?'

'A snivelling Christian he was. Nice workmanship on the cross, though... a pretty thing. Maybe I won't break it, in case their god takes offence. I can sell it to some convert or other for a very high price.'

'And you intend to return and dig your loot up again? How will you remember where it is?'

'Easy. I paced it out, didn't I? Twenty paces north of that plough, then thirty paces west to this fence beside this patch of nettles… Curse it in the name of Woden the One-Eyed! Now I've stung myself. That's your fault for distracting me…'

'Suppose someone moves the plough?'

'I'll kill them, if they do. Oh, no! See on that ridge? [The fellow points] That's Penda and his men. Quick. I must fill in the hole. Go, tell Penda I'm burying my dog… or better still, my aunt. Nobody likes her, the old witch.'

'I'm not going to tell lies to a king as powerful as Penda. You'll have to take your chances, churl, and I'm not sure the odds are in your favour. I'm leaving.'

Phew, that was close. Penda didn't look to be in a good mood. And what a foolish fellow? No wonder he never recovered his treasure hoard.

Books and education

Aelfred passes a law that all men should be allowed time off from their labours to celebrate *Middewinter* on 25 December and the twelve days following. This holiday is rarely called Christmas even though it is revered as the day of Christ's birth. Folk are warned against 'over eating and excess drinking', so you know what to expect – nothing much has changed. Aelfred also insists that folk take two weeks off work for Easter so everyone has the chance to celebrate Christ's resurrection to the full. The king wants even his most humble subjects to understand the basics of the Christian Gospel stories and encourages translations to be made into English. One of the first known plays is performed by monks or clerics to tell of that miraculous moment on Easter morning when the women come to the tomb, discover Christ's body is gone and the angel announces 'He is risen!' And, yes, the men play the women's parts but they are keen to get the message across in whatever way inspires the congregation.

As an adult, as we've heard, Aelfred learns Latin so he can personally check and approve the translations. He always carries a little notebook in which he collects psalms and prayers. His biographer, Bishop Asser, says the book and the king are 'inseparable'. Perhaps Aelfred sees the fabulous *Lindisfarne Gospels*, if he has the opportunity. This book is a spectacular example of an illuminated manuscript and the earliest survivor in England, made in the eighth century by Bishop Eadfrith of Lindisfarne [d. 722]. 'Illuminated' literally means that it shines a light on the words in two ways. Firstly, by decorating the vellum pages with light-reflecting gold and, secondly, by aiding the reader in understanding the meaning of what is written. The main text is in Latin but a word-for-word translation into English is inserted between the lines in the tenth century, maybe inspired by Aelfred's ideas of making the Bible more accessible.

A late Anglo-Saxon colloquy – a sort of play script – is written by a monk, Aelfric, to teach Latin to his pupils. So they can learn the Latin vocabulary and grammar of everyday words, Aelfric makes up a dialogue between tradesmen and craftsmen, arguing about which of them is indispensable. The ploughman says he is because without him there would be no seed planted and, therefore, no food. But the ox-herd says, without him, there would be no oxen to pull the plough. The fisherman says that isn't important because folk can eat his fish.

Not without our skills, say the baker and the cook. Nor without mine, says the carpenter, or else you'll have no boat to go fishing, nor house to live in. You are all wrong, the blacksmith tells them: without me there is no plough, no pots for cooking, no saws or axes to cut wood for building or making ox yokes, no fish-hooks or anything else. It seems the blacksmith has won the argument until the lawyer reminds them that without God, they are all helpless.

Another early literary game which the Anglo-Saxons love is guessing riddles. These are introduced by Hadrian the African who comes to Canterbury in 670 to join his friend Theodore of Tarsus who arrived the year before to take up the post as Archbishop of Canterbury. The two clerics are sent by the pope to raise the standards in the English Church, which is becoming slack in its ways, and to improve education among the Anglo-Saxons. Hadrian is delayed because he's arrested as a spy as he travels through Gaul! Bear this in mind if you show off your education – the authorities are suspicious of clever people.

Probably neither Theodore nor Hadrian speak English but they're both brilliant intellectuals, speaking Greek, Latin and other Mediterranean languages already, so a crash course in English is not too difficult for them. Hadrian is appointed as Abbot of the Abbey of St Peter and St Paul in Canterbury – later known as St Augustine's – where he sets up a school which becomes famous as a place of great learning. Subjects taught include theology, of course, Latin, Greek which has never been studied in England before, astronomy and computing –this means learning how to calculate the correct dates for the Church calendar, rather than coding a new game for your laptop – and poetry.

Poetry includes Latin riddles but Hadrian's students enjoy working out these verbal puzzles so much that they soon start making up their own in English, discovering the language is wonderful for composing these little conundrums. One student, Aldhelm, is inspired by this literary form and writes a collection of a hundred. So are other scholars, including Alcuin and Tatwine. You can play the game too, inventing or guessing riddles but, if you're a sensitive person, I warn you, some are rather risqué. Here's a modest one to get you started:

Great deeds with little strength I do.
I close the open; open the closed for you.
I keep the master's house; the master keeps me too.

Can you guess what it is? The answer is a key.

The Exeter Book is an incredible survivor from these times, containing the majority of the Anglo-Saxon poetry we can still enjoy in the twenty-first century[5]. Most of the texts are unique to the collection which is written up by a single scribe c.950, combining a number of earlier sources into one anthology and, luckily, preserving them for posterity in Exeter Cathedral Library for which we can thank Leofric, the first Bishop of Exeter who died in 1072. His inventory describes it as 'a large English book about many things written in verse'. A selection of almost a hundred riddles or *enigmata* comes at the end – there may have been more but some pages are damaged or missing. This is Riddle 44:

A curiosity hangs by the thigh of a man, under its master's
cloak. It is pierced through in the front; it is stiff and hard
and it has a good standing-place. When the man pulls up
his own robe above his knee, he means to poke with the
head of his hanging thing that familiar hole of matching
length which he has often filled before.

I did warn you that some could be rather lewd but, believe it or not, the answer here is the same as the first riddle: a key.

Apart from the riddles, *The Exeter Book* includes several saints' lives – two about St Guthlac – and tales in verse, most of which are sad elegies about loss, exile and desolation: *The Wanderer* is in search of a new lord after the death of his first, outcast from society and assaulted by the elements. *The Seafarer* is attracted to the wild, untameable sea, something far more powerful than anything experienced on land, equating it to a Christian giving up earthly pleasures to serve the Almighty and sail into a joyous eternity. *The Wife's Lament*, narrated by a woman, and *The Husband's Message* tell the two sides of a story, although there isn't any evidence that they were written as a pair by one poet. The despairing wife has travelled far from her own kin in order to marry but when her husband is exiled as an outlaw, his family drive the wife away, leaving her living in a cave, friendless and alone. The husband's message reminds his wife of their marriage vows, that she must come to him, crossing the sea, no matter the perils, and their joy will be restored. But not all is misery: *The Ruin* is a wonderfully descriptive piece thought to be about the Roman city of Bath. The eighth-century poet is amazed by the stone wall which 'grey with lichen and red of hue, outlives kingdom after kingdom, withstands tempests…' and the anonymous poet is correct because much of that Roman town still stands today.

In a few cases, we know the name of the poet who wrote some of the works in *The Exeter Book*. Cynewulf – though modern scholars aren't sure who he is – composes his poems c.800 and the story of St Juliana, *Christ II* and *The Fates of the Apostles* are all in there. However, Cynewulf's masterpiece *Elene* isn't included. This poem is over 1,300 lines long, telling of St Helena's quest to rescue the remnants of the True Cross from the lands of Islam and spread Christianity throughout the world. St Helena is a popular saint in Anglo-Saxon England because she probably visited Britain. She was wedded to the Roman Emperor Constantius who died in York, hence the connection, if she came with him. Their son, Constantine, became the first emperor to convert to Christianity and force the new religion upon all his subjects throughout the empire. That's the basic story but feel free to embellish it as you wish. That's what *scops* do.

The Exeter Book has a poem entitled *Widsith*. Widsith is a *scop*, travelling across England, telling of legendary heroes, keeping their names alive in poetry and song. It's a lonely life of constant

A man playing a 'tagelharpa'.

wandering but everywhere he goes Widsith is gathering a wealth of new material for his stories and in each mead-hall he 'unlocks his treasury of words' to pass the firelit evening. Maybe he accompanies his tales with the ethereal music of the lyre or perhaps plays the more strident-sounding Viking 'fiddle' or *tagelharpa* which looks rather like the lyre but with only three strings and is played with a horse-hair bow. You can see how the violin evolved from the plucked and strummed lyre. Like the two languages, the Viking instrument makes a much harsher sound than the Anglo-Saxon lyre, but either can provide 'incidental' music to enhance the story telling.

Let's end with a short, cheerful poem, said to have been composed by an illiterate cowherd, Caedmon, who is inspired in a dream to sing this 'hymn'. Since no fewer than seventeen copies of it survive today, it must be extremely popular with Anglo-Saxon audiences:

> *Now we must praise the Guardian of Heaven,*
> *The might of the Lord and His purpose of mind,*
> *The work of the Glorious Father; for He*
> *God Eternal, established each wonder,*
> *He, Holy Creator, first fashioned*
> *Heaven as a roof for the sons of men,*
> *Then the Guardian of Mankind adorned*
> *This middle-earth below, the world for men,*
> *Everlasting Lord, Almighty King.*

I hope you can take ideas from this chapter, enough to help you earn a living and please the people you meet on your journey.

Chapter 9

Warfare

In Anglo-Saxon England, you will have realised by now that warfare is an ever-present possibility, so it may aid you in these threatening times if we take a closer look at how to avoid it and, should that fail, how to improve your chances of surviving a fight.

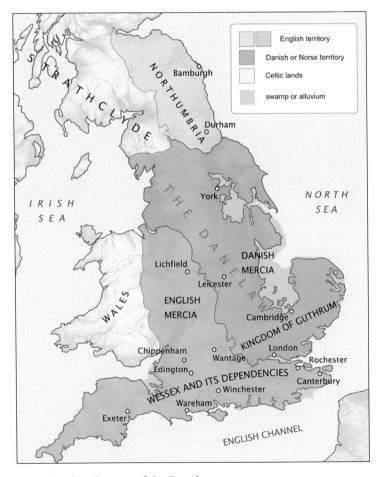

Map showing the area of the Danelaw.

We know that Aelfred does a deal with Guthrum the Dane, dividing England between Wessex in the south and west and the eastern half of the country as far south as the River Thames which becomes known as the Danelaw – literally, the area under Danish law. You may well find that the ordinary folk, whether Anglo-Saxon or Dane, rub along quite well together, farming, trading with each other, living as neighbours and, gradually, combining their two languages into one, doing away with much of the complex grammar in each. Let's hope that the Anglo-Saxons adopt the Viking habit of bathing as well as washing and de-lousing their hair and beards!

Kings and queens

As you might expect, the people at the top on either side aren't entirely happy with the arrangement and always want a bit more of this fertile, wealthy land. Aelfred and his wife Ealhswith have a family of at least two sons and three daughters, not including 'those who were carried off in infancy'. Their first-born, a daughter, Aethelflaed, and the elder son, Eadweard, are crucial to our story.

We heard previously, in 873, that Burghred, King of Mercia, fled to Rome to escape the Danes – an act of cowardice to the Anglo-Saxon way of thinking – and the Danes set up a puppet king, Ceolwulf II, in his place. But Ceolwulf isn't so easily manipulated as the Danes hope and there's the possibility that he may rule Mercia with Aelfred as joint king. Coins have been discovered showing the head of Aelfred

Did You Know?

Ealhswith is never referred to as 'queen' during her lifetime but in death she is described as 'Lady of the English', not just of Wessex, the Anglo-Saxon equivalent of Queen of England. That's quite a posthumous promotion and a sign of things to come.

on one side and Ceolwulf's on the other, suggesting a partnership between Wessex and Mercia, although this isn't noted in the history books. Whatever the truth of the situation, when Ceolwulf II dies, there is no obvious heir to the kingdom of Mercia. Aelfred has lately taken London from the Danes and given it into the care of Ealdorman Aethelred, now his son-in-law since he wed Aethelflaed, Aelfred's eldest daughter. Aethelred is reliable and a good warrior so Aelfred supports him as the new King of Mercia, being acknowledged as Aethelred's overlord as the two kingdoms come ever closer to being united as one. From 886, Aelfred gives himself the impressive title King of the Anglo-Saxons, all of them presumably, so is this a declaration of intent?

Aelfred, his son Eadweard, known as the Elder, and Aethelred are still pitting their wits and fighting the Danes in various combinations. Sometimes it's both kings in arms together, sealing treaties with the enemy. On other occasions, Aethelred and Eadweard are joining forces as at the battle of Farnham in Surrey in 893, when they decisively defeat the Danes while Aelfred is busy doing the same at Exeter in Devon. AD 893 is a pivotal year with Aelfred repeating his rather naïve policy of signing treaties with the enemy and trusting him to keep his word, whereas Haesten, Guthrum's successor as leader of the Viking host from 890, repeatedly and blatantly defaults on the agreements.

Aelfred dies on 26 October 899. He's aged only 50 but has been a martyr to poor health for years. His son, Eadweard the Elder succeeds him but, as you may recall, Aelfred had become king when his elder brother Aethelred I had died, probably of wounds received in battle – too many Aethelreds, I know, just to confuse us – and his sons were too young to take on the job of fighting the Danes. But now cousin Aethelwold, son of Aethelred, is a grown man and challenges Eadweard's right to be king in 902. This is quite acceptable in Anglo-Saxon politics where the best man for the job is more important than who is the direct heir and you can see that Aethelwold has a fair claim to the kingdom anyway. So the matter has to be settled by arms to be certain the better warrior wears the crown. Eadweard wins the day and now sets about solving the Danish problem.

For some years, his brother-in-law, Aethelred of Mercia, has helped Eadweard but he's of the older generation and has been ill for a while. When he dies in 911, Eadweard has a new warrior to fight at his side: Aethelflaed, his sister and Aethelred's widow. Known as 'Lady [or Queen] of the Mercians', although in her forties, she takes up the challenge. Writers at the time don't seem to find this a strange thing for a woman to do, making no particular comments about her as a female warrior. So maybe she is simply the most famous of many but history hasn't recorded the other women who take up arms. However, in later times, with the Normans in charge, Aethelflaed's actions appear unprecedented and heroic. This is what Henry of Huntingdon wrote about her c.1130:

> *Heroic Elflede! Great in martial fame,*
> *A man in valour though a woman in name…*
> *Changed be thy name, such honour triumphs bring.*
> *A queen by title but in deeds a king.*[1]

Even before her husband's death, in 902, Aethelflaed defends Chester from an attack by Norse Vikings sailing from Ireland, restoring the town and setting it on the road to becoming a major trading centre.

In the summer of 910, three Danish 'kings' of Northumbria march south with a huge army, pillaging and plundering their way across

Did You Know?

Reputedly, Aethelflaed drove the Vikings out of Chester by 'covering the enemy in beer' and opening all the beehives in the town so the insects, attracted by the smell of the drink, swarmed and attacked them. Note: the source doesn't say how Aethelflaed succeeded in pouring beer over the Vikings.

Mercia as far as Gloucester, believing Eadweard is occupied in Kent, readying a fleet of a hundred ships to sail north. But Eadweard doesn't linger: he raises troops from both Wessex and Mercia and marches to intercept the Danes whose homeward journey is slowed by the weight of booty they're carrying. Near Wolverhampton, the armies clash and Eadweard wins a stunning victory.

In 917, Aethelflaed again does battle against the Danes, reclaiming the town of Derby from the enemy but she loses 'four thegns who were most dear to her', so it's a hard-fought action. She issues charters and makes grants of land like a king but the coinage of the day bears Eadweard's name. Meanwhile, her brother is fighting the Danes in Northumbria. Together, they push the Danes back beyond the Danelaw boundary. In 918, Aethelflaed successfully takes back Leicester without a fight and her campaigning brings her into contact with the Northumbrians in York, many of whom are Anglo-Saxons. At present, they've given their allegiance to the seemingly all-powerful Danes, not having much choice. But now Aethelflaed may be a good alternative and they offer her – not Eadweard – their loyalty.

But suddenly, in June that year, Aethelflaed dies at Tamworth and her body is later taken to Gloucester and buried beside her husband. Her only child, a daughter, Aelfwynn, succeeds her. The young woman, age uncertain, is formally recognised as Lady of the Mercians but Uncle Eadweard arrives in Tamworth and 'takes to himself the allegiance of all the people of Mercia land that had given allegiance to Aethelflaed'. Aelfwynn is forbidden to marry so there will be no heirs and it's thought she becomes a nun but that's not certain, willingly or not.

But Eadweard can't enjoy his acquired kingdom for long. He dies while on campaign near Chester in July 924. There seems to be some indecision about who should be king after Eadweard. Wessex chooses Aelfweard, the eldest of Eadweard's sons by his first wife, but Mercia opts for Aethelstan. The trouble is that although Aethelstan is the firstborn of Eadweard's children and his mother is probably a Mercian noblewoman, Ecgwynn, his parents never married. But because he is raised in Mercia by his aunt, Aethelflaed, he's the preferred choice there. Matters seem to sort themselves out – very conveniently – when Aelfweard dies a couple of weeks later but now Wessex promotes Aelfweard's brother, the teenager, Eadwin. Arguments rumble on for more than a year after their father's death and there's rumour of an attempt on Aethelstan's life shortly before his long-delayed coronation on 4 September 925.

As a visitor to Anglo-Saxon England, you won't want to miss this grand occasion which takes place at Kingston-upon-Thames, west of London, the event that makes Aethelstan the undisputed King of the Anglo-Saxons of both Wessex and Mercia. Anointed with holy oil, invested with the royal regalia of a ring, sword, crown, sceptre and staff, he makes a promise in three parts: to keep the peace, forbid wrong-doing by high and low alike and to promote justice and mercy through the rule of law. Then he is shown to the people that they may know and recognise him. As for the doubters among the West Saxons, he will prove they did well to change their minds: the crown is in safe hands.

What Aethelstan achieves during just ten months, between July 927 and April 928, is incredible. He conquers Britain! Within three generations – from Aelfred to his son Eadweard and daughter Aethelflaed and now his grandson Aethelstan – St Cuthbert's prophesy made to Aelfred at his lowest ebb in Athelney has come true: his descendants rule all England. Yet some versions of the *Anglo-Saxon*

Did You Know?

A copy of the order of service used for Aethelstan's coronation still exists in the National Library in Paris, France, showing he was crowned as 'King of the Anglo-Saxons'. A Gospel Book kept at the British Library in London records that, after the ceremony, the king gave a slave, Eadhelm, and his children their freedom for 'the good of his soul'.

Chronicle almost airbrush Aethelstan from history because he's illegitimate and not Wessex's first choice.

Briefly, Aethelstan goes to war against all the other kings and leading warriors in the land. He subdues Constantin, King of Scots; Owain, King of the Strathclyde Welsh, the Chiefs of Alba and Pictland; Guthfrith, the Danish King of York, the Anglian Lords of Bamburgh and a number of Anglo-Danish jarls [earls]. All pay him tribute, giving him valuable gifts and hostages for their good behaviour – standard requirements at the time. Aethelstan is now overlord of more of this island than the Romans managed to conquer but he isn't finished yet. The Western 'Welsh' of Cornwall claim his attention next but he doesn't come as a warlord but as a benefactor of religious houses and churches, setting in place a Bishopric of Cornwall and rebuilding Exeter.

Now it's the turn of Wales itself and there's no soft touch here: this is a clash of arms. Hywel Dda, King of North Wales, Idwal Foel, King of Gwynedd and three kings from central and southern Wales are forced to come to terms with Aethelstan at Hereford. The extent of their defeat is reflected in the enormous size of the annual payments of tribute he demands of them: twenty pounds weight of gold; three hundred pounds weight of silver; 25,000 oxen and as many hawks and hounds as he desires.

Aethelstan reigns supreme over the entire island! Something never achieved before nor since until the eighteenth century.

Six years of peace and prosperity follow. It's time to put the kingdom straight. New ideas, innovations and experiments in methods of government are introduced. Though not all of them work out, many become the foundations of governing England to this day. Keen to revise and enforce the law of this huge kingdom, Aethelstan summons his thegns to a great gathering to discuss the matter. Christian morals have to be balanced against the reality of savage lawlessness. The death sentence has become a standard punishment and, in theory, the preferred deterrent since Christianity was embraced. The adopted religion regards punishing the offender for the good of his soul as being more important than compensating the victim and his family, the way it used to be in the old law codes. But Aethelstan has his merciful moments and on seeing a young lad hanged for 'so small an offence', the king raises the lower age limit on capital punishment from twelve to fifteen years.

The king is not only keen to improve the way England is governed. Living in towns or burhs within fortified walls is becoming more of an option since Aethelstan's grandfather, Aelfred, began his policy of town-planning. Within the safety of these towns, the king sets up mints to produce silver pennies which are so pure and reliable that England's coinage system is the envy of Europe. Trade flourishes, merchants are doing well and fledgling craft guilds are first seen in this reign. Aethelstan has time to reform religion too, reviving bishoprics, repairing monasteries that have suffered Viking attacks and checking on standards of pastoral care in the community. One scribe noted 'there was peace and abundance in all things'. Aethelstan has special 'crown-wearing' occasions to remind everyone he is the most successful King of England – ever. Foreign rulers are also suitably impressed but, of course, it cannot last.

All those sub-kings who have been forced to pay tributes make a concerted effort to grab back their full authority. There are rebellions by the Scots, the Welsh and the Danes of Dublin in Ireland join this Celtic uprising in the summer of 937, devastating the north of England. Aethelstan must be annoyed and disappointed that his efforts aren't universally appreciated – time to put these ungrateful lesser kings in their place.

It's a bloody clash at Brunanburh in the early winter of that year. This battle site isn't known for certain in the twenty-first century but

 Top Tip

A pound weight of silver coins is worth £1. This is more money than the average churl will ever see.

may well be Bromborough, across the River Mersey from modern day Liverpool [which doesn't exist at the time]. Losses on both sides are terrible. King Constantin of Scots loses his sons and Aethelstan's cousins are slain. But the English have the victory and, at the time, Brunanburh is spoken of as the 'Great Battle'.

We've heard that Aethelstan wasn't a legitimate son of his father, King Eadweard, and it seems he accepts the fact that he is only the 'caretaker' monarch because he never marries and has no direct heir. When he dies only two years after the battle – ironically, outlived by Constantin and the other rebel leaders – in October 939, he chooses to be buried at Malmesbury Abbey, rather than at Winchester with his royal forbears. He is succeeded by his father's legitimate sons, first Edmund, then Eadred, followed by Edmund's sons, Eadwig and Eadgar. Which brings us to 959.

Peace in our time

If you wish to visit Anglo-Saxon England and hope to avoid being caught up in warfare, Eadgar's reign [959-75] is the safest time to come. He is known as Eadgar the Peaceable, not because he does everything possible to avoid fighting but because no enemies dare to challenge the might of England.

The Vikings stay at home, busy squabbling amongst themselves, while England, with her battle renown, her war-ready fleet of ships and hardy warriors with victories behind them, stands unchallenged.

Eadgar has the leisure to continue Uncle Aethelstan's coinage

A coin of King Eadgar.

reforms, bringing the minting system under tighter, personal control and standardising the coins themselves. The coiners who make them have to include their name or maker's mark and the town where they're produced into the design so the king knows who to blame – and punish – if coins are discovered to be underweight or dodgy in anyway. They are also a great way of advertising himself to all his subjects and anyone else who sees the coins as they proclaim him: 'Eadgar King of the English' in the legend surrounding his image.

He reorganises the country under four principal ealdordoms – Mercia, East Anglia and Northumbria with himself in overall command and holding Wessex. The ealdordoms are then divided into shires – most of which are still recognisable as today's counties – and dioceses are rearranged with some new bishops appointed. Like his uncle before him, Eadgar encourages the reform, the re-founding of old religious communities and the foundation of new ones and he has two future saints to assist and advise him: Dunstan, Archbishop of Canterbury, and Aethelwold, Abbot of Abingdon and Bishop of Winchester. Wealthy families climb on the band-wagon, pouring resources into the Church, hoping to guarantee their places in heaven.

After fourteen years on the throne, Eadgar feels it's time for a second, grand coronation in Bath. Everyone of any importance is invited and this is what the *Anglo-Saxon Chronicle* has to say about the event:

> *Here Eadgar, ruler of the English,*
> *Was consecrated as king, among a great crowd*
> *In the ancient city ...*
> *... There was great bliss*
> *For everyone on that blessed day,*
> *Which the sons of men name and call*
> *Pentecost Day. There was a crowd of priests,*
> *A great throng of monks, I have heard,*
> *A gathering of the wise. ...*

And he, Edmund's heir, had
Nine and twenty winters in the world,
Doughty in war-work, when this was done,
And in the thirtieth was consecrated lord.

Unlike his uncle who never took a wife, Eadgar marries three times. By his first wife he has a son, Edward, born before Eadgar becomes king. I can't discover what happened to wife number one; maybe she died in childbirth. After he accedes to the throne, Eadgar marries Wulfthryth who gives him a daughter, Eadith, before retiring to become a nun and, eventually, Abbess of Wilton Abbey. Eadith follows her mother to Wilton, later serving as abbess and becoming a saint. Now although he's still officially wed to Wulfthryth, Eadgar decides he needs a wife at his side. Aelfthryth becomes wife number three and gives him two more sons, Edmund, who dies as a child, and Aethelred.

In July 975, King Eadgar's sudden and unexpected death shocks everyone, cause unknown. Edward, the eldest child, becomes king but things don't go well. In 976, quarrels erupt among the leading ealdormen, some newly appointed by Edward. Then, in 978, at a meeting of the leading members of the king's council in an upstairs chamber, the floor collapses, killing and injuring many of Edward's most important supporters. Queen Aelfthryth, Eadgar's widow, wants her remaining son, Aethelred, to wear the crown although he is still too young to rule in person.

In March 978, King Edward visits Corfe Castle in Dorset. It hasn't been a good year so far for him and it's about to get worse. Nobody knows for certain who is the guilty party – unless you can unravel the mystery – but Edward is murdered. Since she and her son have most to gain from her stepson's death, Queen Aelfthryth seems the most likely mover and shaker behind the scenes of this act of regicide, if not the actual perpetrator. Poor Edward is given a hasty burial in the nearest church, St Martin's in Wareham, although he is later reburied at Shaftesbury Abbey, to become known to posterity as Edward 'the Martyr'.

And it's downhill all the way from here for Anglo-Saxon England.

Corfe Castle, scene of King Edward's murder.

The 'unready' king

Aethelred is about twelve years old when he has his rushed coronation at Kingston-upon-Thames as King Aethelred II so he isn't in charge. His mother is powerful in the early days but political plots and schemes riddle the court. In later, popular history, he becomes Ethelred the Unready and he definitely isn't ready for what happens during his reign. However, his contemporaries call him 'the Unraed' which means the 'uncounselled' or, as we might say, 'ill-advised'. But it's always safest to blame a king's mistakes on his advisors, rather than the man himself – a fact that remains true throughout history. Is he given poor advice or, more likely in a youngster suddenly presented with vast wealth and power, does he choose to ignore the wisdom of older and wiser men? Whatever the case, England suffers the consequences.

Aethelred II is king for two years and it's only five years since Eadgar's death when England looked to be safe from any enemies but the Vikings can smell a weak kingdom from the other side of the North Sea. They know England is wealthy and has been at peace for decades. Have her warriors grown old; her administration slow and cumbersome, concerned with matters other than military defence?

In 980, they decide to try their luck. One fleet of Viking longships raid the Isle of Thanet in Kent and then Southampton on the south coast, abbeys and churches being the main, soft targets, as usual. A second fleet attacks Cheshire from the Irish Sea. In 981, it's Devon and Cornwall which suffer and London is ravaged in 982.

The method by which the Anglo-Saxons marshal their forces to defend against marauders can leave them vulnerable. It's the responsibility of the shire *fyrd* to deal with local raids and although the king can call up the national militia to defend the kingdom, problems with communication and raising supplies means that the army cannot be mustered very quickly. Only after the enemy has landed does the summons go out to ealdormen and thegns to gather their men for battle. Large areas can be devastated before the *fyrd* is assembled and

Did You Know?

The tale is told that at Aethelred's christening, the omens are bad. As Archbishop Dunstan lowers the infant Aethelred into the font – babies were immersed in those times – he does a poo in the holy water. It's not a good sign and Dunstan declares the child will be an ignoble man.

marching to repel the attack, so it's often down to the men on the spot to do the best they can.

In 986, there is a new King of Denmark, Swein Forkbeard. There is also a new leader of the Norwegian Vikings, Olaf Tryggvason. In 991, Olaf arrives with a fleet of almost a hundred ships. After briefly terrorising East Kent, Olaf lands at Maldon in Essex, not far from Prittlewell [see Chapter 8]. There, the Norse invaders are met by Ealdorman Byrhtnoth, an ageing war veteran and his loyal band. They are mostly warriors in the old style, faithful to the last and regarding death at their lord's side as honourable. Surrender or flight are not options. Byrhtnoth and his men know they are outnumbered but when the enemy's messenger offers to leave in peace upon the payment of tribute in gold, this is what the old warrior shouts back, according to the heroic poem about the battle of Maldon:

> *Can you hear, you pirate, what these people say?*
> *They will pay you a tribute of whistling spears,*
> *Of deadly darts and proven swords,*
> *Weapons to pay you, pierce, slit*
> *And slay you in the storm of battle…*
> *Break the news to your people*
> *That a noble earl and his troop stand here –*
> *Guardians of the people and the country,*
> *Home of Aethelred my prince –*
> *Who will defend this land to the last ditch.*[2]

And that's exactly what Byrhtnoth does even as 'the slaughter-wolves' cut him down and slay him. Many of his men die at his side. As Leofsunu declares: 'I will not retreat so much as one foot but will go forward and avenge my lord in battle'. But Godric, the cowardly son of Odda, along with his brothers, Godwine and Godwig, gallop away and save themselves, betraying their lord. However, a long list of named champions stand firm, including another Godric – this the son of Aethelgar, as the poet is quick to point out – who 'gave them heart to continue the fight' but all is in vain. Avoid Maldon, if you hope to survive and life could become unpleasant if you're named as a coward and betrayer, like Odda's sons. Best keep well away, if I were you.

All versions of *The Anglo-Saxon Chronicles* generally give Aethelred a bad press while modern research is suggesting that maybe he isn't as bad as the chronicles make out. But one fact can't be overlooked: Aethelred avoids leading the English into battle, despite numerous opportunities to do so during the 990s, when he is in his late twenties and early thirties. At that age, any Anglo-Saxon warrior worthy of his name should be facing the Viking threat head on, sword in hand. But Aethelred appoints ealdormen to do the task for him. It's a good survival strategy but no wonder the people – and the chroniclers – are disappointed and unimpressed by this king. Yet he has reason not to take unnecessary risks in that there are no close, adult male relatives to replace him if he's killed and his children are still too young. However, among the ealdormen given command of the *fyrd* none are of the calibre of old Byrhtnoth. Ealdorman Aelfric, for example, when facing the Danish army at Exeter, pretends he is too sick to fight and abandons his men, hiding in his tent.

There are a number of clashes with the Vikings, most of which see the Anglo-Saxons coming off worst so it seems a good idea to pay them to go away. In 991, after Maldon, the king pays £10,000 in *danegeld* to Olaf Tryggvason and then, in 994, Swein Forkbeard joins forces with Olaf, so the situation isn't improving. Another £16,000 payment of *danegeld* is no deterrent. The Vikings must be laughing over their mead. London is their particular target and the only objective seems to be total destruction and devastation. The writer of one version of *The Anglo-Saxon Chronicles* seems to be living in the city at the time and describes the Londoners' heroic struggles to defend it against repeated attacks, year after year. 'Praise be to God it still stands', he notes.

In 1011, another Viking leader, Thorkell the Tall and his horde destroy and occupy Canterbury, taking Archbishop Aelfheah hostage. Aethelred's counsellors raise an incredible sum – £48,000 – to ransom him but the archbishop forbids them to pay a penny for his

---

Did You Know?

On St Bryce Day, the 13 November 1002, Aethelred orders the massacre of every Dane in the country. Of course, his order is ignored throughout the Danelaw but innocent civilian Danes whose families have lived here for generations are murdered in Oxford and Weymouth and probably elsewhere.

---

safe return. His captors, drunk on wine, throw things at him until one strikes him with an axe. Aelfheah is martyred and buried in St Paul's, London since Canterbury Cathedral is in enemy hands.

To cut a long story short... in 1013, Swein Forkbeard returns in force. England is overrun. King Aethelred sends his wife, Emma of Normandy, and their sons to safety at her brother's court in Normandy and Aethelred follows them into exile soon after Christmas. By default, Swein the Dane is now King of England but he dies at the beginning of February 1014. His army chooses his son, twenty-year-old Cnut, to be king. The English urge Aethelred to return which he does, catching Cnut off guard so he takes to his ships. However, a huge Danish army still occupies Greenwich, then in Kent, near London and another £21,000 *danegeld* payment doesn't persuade them to leave. Aethelred and his eldest son, Edmund, quarrel about the lack of action against the enemy and Edmund wants to make a stand but the powerful English earls, like Eadric Streona of Mercia, known as 'the Grasper', are taking Cnut's side.

In the spring of 1015, Aethelred the Unraed dies. The Witan in London elects Edmund as King of England and he's made of stouter stuff than his father. Known as 'Ironside', young Edmund raises the *fyrd* and goes into battle, repeatedly and successfully, his infantry forming shield walls in the Anglo-Saxon traditional way of fighting. He regains London and chases Cnut back into Kent where they clash at the battle of Otford. Cnut tries to hold his ground but when Edmund and his men charge them, the Danes panic and flee.

An Anglo-Saxon shield wall.

Is this a new beginning for Anglo-Saxon England? I wish it was.

On the 18 October 1016, Edmund Ironside and Cnut face each other for the decisive challenge at Assandun, Essex. Edmund, full of confidence after five successive victories, goes on the attack immediately. This tactic has worked so well previously but then Edmund wasn't relying on Eadric Streona of Mercia. As the two armies exchange the first sword thrusts, Eadric leaves the field, taking his sizable Mercian contingent with him, betraying his king – 'as he had done many times'. It's said that this act of treachery was planned beforehand between Eadric and Cnut. As a result, 'all the flower of England perished there', at Assandun. But Edmund survives, raises more troops and determines to fight on. Eventually, he and Cnut agree to rule the country between them: Edmund to reign in Wessex and Cnut to have the rest. They're sworn to be 'as brothers', in which case Edmund's convenient death within a month of the agreement is most probably fratricide.

Cnut is now declared to be 'King of All the English', yet, in the time-honoured Viking fashion, he demands the immediate payment of *danegeld*: £72,000 with an extra £10,500 to be paid by the Londoners alone. This is reckoned to amount to 20 million silver pennies!

England is now a province of Denmark; no longer ruled by Anglo-Saxon kings. And thus it remains for twenty-five years, so let us move on.

Chapter 10

The End of the Anglo-Saxon Era

Danish Kings of England

At King Cnut's court there is a man named Godwine. His father, Wulfnoth, was a Sussex thegn wrongly accused by Aethelred in 1008, so he decided to support the Danes. His son, Godwine, benefits and becomes one of Cnut's most important counsellors and military leaders. In return, Cnut makes him Earl of Wessex. The other powerful earls appointed by Cnut are Siward of Northumbria and Leofric of Mercia.

Godwine accumulates wealth and power across southern England and acquires a royal bride, Gytha, Cnut's sister-in-law. Of their large family of six sons and three daughters, the three eldest boys are all given Danish names: Swein, Harold and Tostig, probably to keep favour with the king. The youngest three boys though are given English names: Gyrth, Leofwine and Wulfnoth; as are their daughters: Edith [Eadgyth], Aelfgifu, although Gunhild sounds Danish but the suffix '…hild' isn't unknown among Anglo-Saxon girls' names, as in St Hild[a], Abbess of Whitby. The Godwines are a bi-lingual family, more Anglo-Danish than Anglo-Saxon.

Around this time, after a terrible famine throughout Europe in 1005, known as 'the Great Hunger', the weather improves

 Top Tip

The Danish version of an ealdorman is a 'jarl', so the title of 'earl' is a compromise between the two languages.

generally. Famine becomes less of a threat as the climate warms up. This is fortunate for the wife of Leofric, Earl of Mercia. Her name is Godgifu – literally 'God's gift' – but you may know her better as Lady Godiva, famous for riding naked through the streets of Coventry. The story goes that she wanted her husband to reduce or even abolish the taxes and fees he was forcing the townsfolk to pay which they couldn't afford. Leofric agreed that he would on condition that she rode from one end of the town to the other, through the marketplace, without her clothes. He was probably laughing as he dared her, certain she would do no such thing. But Godgifu called his bluff. She let down her long hair, her abundant tresses being enough to cover her modesty, mounted her horse and did as he dared her. Leofric had to keep his word and Coventry became a tax-free haven. We have no idea if this really happened as the story doesn't appear until much later but it's a gem of a tale for the Anglo-Saxon *scop*.

King Cnut has two wives at the same time. Is this illegal? It seems not. His first wife is Aelfgifu of Northampton who gives him two sons, Swein and Harald. In 1017, Cnut marries Emma of Normandy, King Aethelred's widow, although Aelfgifu is still alive. Emma is old enough to be Cnut's mother but she's important and boosts his claim to the throne. Having two wives is nothing new. King Eadgar did the same and it seems that although a man already has a wife, becoming king wipes the slate clean, so he can marry again. In both cases, because wife number two weds a king, *she* becomes queen. Apparently, as Cnut marries Emma with full Christian rites, the Church accepts this marriage as the official union, whereas he only wed Aelfgifu 'by Danish custom'. I'm unsure what Danish custom entails but, later on, Harold Godwineson will marry Edith Swan-neck in this manner and later take another woman in a political marriage to be his queen.

Meanwhile, Queen Emma, who already has two sons from her first marriage to King Aethelred, Alfred and Edward, now gives birth to Cnut's son, Harthacnut, his father's designated heir but by far the youngest of all the possible contestants for the throne: Alfred and Edward, Emma's sons by Aethelred; Swein and Harald [known as 'Harefoot' for reasons we do not know], Aelfgifu's sons by Cnut and Harthacnut, Emma's son by Cnut.

Although only in his thirties, Cnut dies unexpectedly in November 1035, of natural causes, so it's said. His first wife, Aelfgifu, and their eldest son, Swein, have been in Norway for the last five years, then move to Denmark where Swein promptly goes the way of his father. Emma's sons, Alfred and Edward, are in Normandy and Harthacnut is also in Denmark so the only available candidate for kingship is Aelfgifu's son, Harald Harefoot. Perhaps, if you meet him you can discover the reason for his nickname. Queen Emma and Earl Godwine try to set up a regency council to rule on behalf of the absent Harthacnut but an alternative faction led by Earl Leofric of Mercia supports Harald Harefoot. At first, they too propose only an alternative, Mercian regency until Harthacnut comes home but because Harald is here, already in England, he claims the throne as King Harald or Harold I. After all, a kingdom without a king is always at risk and Harthacnut isn't in a hurry to leave Denmark. This is bad news for Queen Emma, Earl Godwine and the Wessex faction.

Since her boy Harthacnut doesn't seem eager to rule England, Emma sends for her sons by Aethelred to come from Normandy, known as the Athelings. Edward arrives in England first, at Southampton, planning to meet his mother at her base in Winchester where, conveniently, the royal treasury is kept. But instead of a rapturous welcome, he's met by an army and swiftly returns to Normandy. Meanwhile, Alfred, the younger of the two, lands at Dover, also intending to go to his mother. However, he's met by Earl Godwine on route. The earl swears allegiance to Alfred and escorts him and his followers to Guildford in Surrey. There, the earl throws a party to welcome the Atheling home. Alfred and his men go to bed, somewhat drunk but happy with their lavish reception. But it's all a ruse.

Godwine remains a staunch supporter of Cnut's son, Harald and, supposedly on his orders, the earl attacks his sleeping guests. Alfred's men are either killed outright, mutilated or taken captive, to be sold as slaves. Alfred himself is dragged to London and brought before Harald. The king commands that his rival is taken away and his eyes are to be put out. Rumour has it that Godwine does the horrible deed and the unfortunate, blinded Atheling later dies of his injuries. The chroniclers call it 'murder'. As for Emma, having attempted to put her sons on the throne, she's accounted a traitor and flees to Bruges in Flanders.

By 1037, King Harald is accepted throughout the country and he and Godwine are triumphant but this is Anglo-Saxon England where good fortune rarely lasts long. In March 1040, Harald dies suddenly, leaving a small son, Aelfwine [an Anglo-Saxon name], as his heir who would later become a monk. Emma has been joined at last by Harthacnut in Bruges and they are currently planning an invasion but, with Harald gone, nobody opposes them and Harthacnut is welcomed as king. The body of Harald is exhumed from its grave in Westminster Abbey and flung into the nearby marsh. Godwine is accused of having murdered the new king's half-brother, Alfred, but buys his sovereign's favour with a stupendous gift: a huge, eighty-man warship with all the trimmings and accoutrements.

Harthacnut is out for revenge against the people who had accepted Harald as king instead of waiting for his long-delayed return. Although, initially, his subjects greet him with enthusiasm, his immediate demand that they give him £21,099 to pay the expenses

---

🔖 Top Tip

If you fall foul of a king, an expensive present may well regain his friendship. Bribery is a good survival strategy.

of his would-be invasion fleet and then the imposition of swingeing taxation don't endear him to anyone. The shire of Worcester is ravaged on Harthacnut's orders after two of his tax-collectors are killed by disgruntled townsfolk. Men are murdered with his knowledge, even while guaranteed the king's safe conduct.

Sometime in the early months of 1042, Harthacnut invites his half-brother, Edward, to come from Normandy to rule as his co-king. Historians aren't sure why. Some suggest that Harthacnut may have been suffering with a long-term illness, such as tuberculosis, and wanted to ensure the succession since he had no children. Others think he was planning to invade Denmark to retake his father's kingdom there and wanted a non-threatening regent to rule in his absence since he didn't wholly trust Earls Godwine, Leofric or Sirward. Or it could have been a trick to get his remaining rival into his hands and deal with him once and for all.

Whatever the reason, Edward accepts the invitation. At the time, Normandy is in chaos, so he's probably pleased to leave. Whether he might have come to regret his decision, if Harthacnut had some devious scheme in mind, we shall never know, because he had only just arrived at court when, on 8 June 1042, Harthacnut attends a wedding in Lambeth, across the River Thames from London. Both the bride and groom are high born and it's a great occasion but, as the king drinks to the health of the happy couple, as the chronicler records:

> *Harthacnut died as he stood at his drink and he suddenly fell to the earth with an awful convulsion; and those who were close by took hold of him, and he spoke no word afterwards...*

Historians have speculated that he suffered a stroke or a brain haemorrhage but one at least is certain that he was poisoned 'but the culprit will never be known with certainty due to there being no shortage of discontented candidates'[1].

The return of the English

Edward is here in England, just handy for the Witan to promote him as king. Officially, he is King Edward II but he becomes better known to history as Edward the Confessor. Edward is anointed and crowned at Winchester on Easter Sunday, 1043, the city chosen deliberately to show the king is of the original royal line of Wessex without any Danish blood – unless you count his mother, Emma of Normandy, whose family were the 'Norsemen' or Normans, descendants of the Viking, Rollo. In any case, Edward wants nothing to do with his mother since she has promoted, in turn, every other member of the family as king except him, despite his being King Aethelred's eldest son.

Earl Godwine, as usual determined to be on the winning side, supports Edward wholeheartedly but the feeling isn't mutual. Edward hasn't forgotten that this man was responsible for the death of his brother Alfred, but he needs him as an ally and to command armies – something of which Edward has little or no experience. For a decade, Godwine and the king work together, Edward taking the earl's daughter, Edith, as his wife, but it's a wary alliance, neither quite trusting the other.

England is a very prosperous place in the mid-eleventh century. By this time, there are more than a hundred thriving towns in England with up to one-tenth of the population living in these urban centres and no longer working the land as their main means of earning a living. Instead, these town-dwellers are relying to some extent on others growing food for them. So now markets develop as places where money is exchanged for food and other commodities can be bought and sold. Of course, the king and the Church want their share of the profits and charge tolls and fees for setting up a stall and, perhaps, for crossing the bridge to reach the market. Towns are also handy centres for tax-gathering and the system is well organised and efficient. It has to be, otherwise collecting those incredible sums to pay *danegeld* would be impossible.

There's a lot going on in an Anglo-Saxon town as this marvellous poem, *The Gifts of Mortals,* tells us in these excerpts as it celebrates the great variety of skills given to man by a benevolent God:

> *One can devise a wonderful contrivance –*
> *something timbered, tall – his hand is well-taught,*
> *skilful and steady, just as is proper for the wright,*
> *establishing the hall, he knows how to conjoin*
> *the broad house firmly against its sudden fall.* (lines 41-48)

> *One can address the harp with his hands –*
> *he has the art of swift striking the joyful wood.*
> *One is skilful at counsel, another steady in aim,*
> *another perceptive in poetry, another swift on land,*
> *quick on his feet. One steers the till[er] on the fallow wave,*
> *knowing the streaming road, the course of armies,*
> *over the broad ocean, when the sea-eager are shaken*
> *with swift power of the oars, near to the wave-board.*
>   (lines 49-57)

> *One is a good swimmer. Another crafty in artifice*
> *of gold and gemstones, when the Warden of Men*
> *commands him to adorn them as glorious treasures.*
> *One can make warlike tackle, useful to warriors,*
> *a mind-crafty smith, when he creates a helmet*
> *or a dagger or a warlike jacket for the battles of men;*
> *a shining sword or the boss of a shield,*
> *brought together surely against the flying of spears.*
>   (lines 58-66)

> *One is pious and eager to give alms –*
> *virtuous in his habits. Another is an active thane*
> *in the mead-hall. One is well-versed in steeds,*
> *wise in horsemanship. Another is wise in books,*
> *limb-strong in learning. Still another is*
> *hand-ready in the writing of wordy mysteries.* (lines 86-96)

Many of these skills can only flourish when wrights [workers of wood], smiths [workers of metal] and other artisans have time to spare from growing crops and rearing livestock to learn the art of their craft, improve techniques and develop ideas. Living in towns enables this to happen. In the 1040s-1060s, the Godwine family own properties in thirty-seven different towns across the kingdom in addition to their vast land-holdings as earls. They are certainly the wealthiest people in the country but there are numerous folk who are almost as rich.

Earl Godwine's eldest son, Swein, is described as 'wild'. He claims that King Cnut was his father, not Godwine, though his mother vehemently denies this. King Edward creates Swein Earl of Somerset and Berkshire – taken from Godwine's earldom – and Gloucestershire, Herefordshire and Oxfordshire taken from Leofric of Mercia. The second son, Harold, is made Earl of East Anglia and Godwine's Danish nephew, Beorn, is given an earldom in the Danelaw part of Mercia. But Swein wants more and joins the Welsh kings in revolt against Edward. It's said that he rapes the Abbess of Leominster while in the Welsh borderlands. Both Church and nobility are disgusted at such behaviour and the king outlaws him and splits the miscreant's earldom between Harold and Beorn as Swein flees to Denmark.

In 1050, Swein is back, asking Edward's forgiveness with opposition from cousin Beorn and his brother Harold, both of whom had benefitted from Swein's confiscated earldom and lands. His sister,

---

Did You Know?

If you are outlawed – or, if a woman, you are 'waived' – you are outside the protection of the law. You can be hunted down and killed like a wild beast and your killer can claim a reward if he presents your head to the authorities. Hence the alternative name for an outlaw: a 'wolf's-head' because the same applies to wolves.

Queen Edith, ignores him but he's partially reinstated. Beorn is a Danish prince with a reasonable claim to the kingdom of Denmark and possibly has his eye on the English crown too as an heir to Cnut. Godwine and his son, Swein, decide to take matters into their own hands, as a 'favour' to the childless King Edward? Who knows? The pair abduct Beorn and kill him which becomes an international diplomatic incident. Edward has to be seen to take action against Godwine and his family who are forced to flee the country. Swein goes on a pilgrimage to Jerusalem to earn forgiveness for murdering his cousin and dies on the way back.

But if Edward is relieved, it's short-lived because Godwine returns with a fleet of ships, an army and the invaluable support of the wealthy Londoners. Edward gives in, reinstates the family and accepts Edith back as his queen but it's Godwine who now rules England in all but name from 1052. The king's court is celebrating Easter 1053 at Winchester with a good dinner when Earl Godwine collapses. He lingers for a few days but doesn't recover. The symptoms sound like those of a stroke – just as Harthacnut suffered in similar circumstances – but at the royal court you can never tell. And Edward has no chance to snatch back his regal powers because Godwine's son, Harold, steps straight into the gap left by his father's death. Godwine is buried in kingly splendour in Winchester Old Minster alongside Cnut, Harthacnut and Beorn, all of Danish blood.

Harold is now the all-powerful Earl of Wessex, passing his own earldom of East Anglia to his younger brother, Gyrth. In 1055, when

Did You Know?

Harold leads an army to victory against King Macbeth in Scotland in 1054. This is the famous scene in Shakespeare's play where the witches prophesy that Macbeth will be king 'till Birnam Wood do come to Dunsinane', until the English army come camouflaged by tree branches.

King Edward the Confessor and Earl Harold Godwineson.

Siward, the Earl of Northumbria dies leaving a child as his heir, Harold makes certain his brother, Tostig, gets the job with Queen Edith's support. Earl Leofric of Mercia, once a significant balance for the Godwines, is now surrounded by them on all sides. When he dies in 1057, Harold and his close kin are lords of all.

Harold is reckoned a skilful warrior – unlike his father who usually managed to avoid outright conflict – taking on both the Scots and the Welsh. He is also a successful diplomat, negotiating treaties with foreign rulers while Edward takes a back seat. Harold has two more brothers in this large family. The next brother down the line is Leofwine and, since he now holds so much of England, Harold gives him lands on both sides of the Thames estuary, in Kent and Essex, and Edward approves this as a new earldom for Leofwine. The remaining Godwineson is the youngest, Wulfnoth, who has drawn the short straw at every turn. Way back, when King Edward pledged peace with Normandy, hostages were exchanged as was the custom. Wulfnoth was one of those hostages. Maybe Harold could pull a few diplomatic strings to get his little brother released but, if he does, history didn't record the fact. Neither does it note how Wulfnoth was treated nor when he died. Poor Wulfnoth.

For Tostig, now Earl of Northumbria, things aren't going so well either. As a man of Wessex, he is unpopular with the local thegns who were hoping to be in charge after Siward's death. Tostig deals with some of the most prominent noblemen in the usual way: by killing them. When he then imposes swingeing taxes and a host of unfamiliar West-Saxon laws, by 1065 he has a rebellion on his hands. The rebels are aided by Edwin, the new Earl of Mercia, and Tostig hopes his brother Harold will help him deal with the threat. But to Tostig's great disappointment, Harold agrees with the Northumbrians about the taxes. Tostig is deprived of his earldom and flees the country, holding an enormous grudge against Harold. Edwin's brother, Morcar, is created Earl of Northumbria instead, the locals' preferred choice.

On Christmas Day of that year, King Edward carries out his customary duties but on the next day, he takes to his bed. Known as 'the Confessor' because of his piety and saintly ways – which may have included not sleeping with his wife, Edith, or any other women – Edward dies on 4-5 January 1066. Edith, Harold and

---

📌 Top Tip

Make yourself inconspicuous whenever hostages are being selected as matters may not end well.

Stigund, Archbishop of Canterbury, are at his bedside but, of course, there are no royal offspring to succeed the dying king. As in the past, the Witan chooses the most suitable, available candidate and who else can it be? Harold exchanges his earldom for the crown. Some say Edward nominated his brother-in-law; others that he intended William, Duke of Normandy, to succeed him, being grateful to the Normans for keeping him safe in exile there. It's true Edward had little to do with England before 1042. There wasn't much love lost between him and his noblemen and most of his Church appointments went to foreigners. Was Edward not bothered about continuing the line of Anglo-Saxon kings? Can you answer this question for us?

Harold's kingship is challenged by the northern earls, the brothers Edwin and Morcar, but instead of making a fight of it, Harold marries their sister, Edith of Mercia, and all is well.

All through the summer of 1066, Tostig is making a nuisance of himself along the east coast, doing battle with Earl Edwin at one point. However, in September, he tries again, this time with major back-up from King Harald Hardrada of Norway who has a fancy to be King of England as well. Tostig has the same idea but, for now, the two are allies. They arrive with their combined fleet and warrior host, disembarking on the Yorkshire shore of the River Humber on 18 September. Two days later, they do battle with the armies of Edwin and Morcar at Fulford. The English are hugely outnumbered and outmanoeuvred and although both earls survive, it's a great victory for Tostig and Hardrada. The city of York surrenders to Hardrada and

Did You Know?

Harold already has a wealthy, land-owner wife, Edith Swan-neck. (Too many Ediths, I know!) They've been together for about twenty years and have at least five children. But Harold married her by the Danish custom, so the Church doesn't count it as a legal union and he's free to wed a 'true' wife.

the Norwegians set up camp a few miles away at Stamford Bridge and settle down to some serious celebrating. It's a mistake.

Meanwhile, King Harold has spent the summer on the south coast with his army, expecting an invasion from Normandy, aware that Duke William has been busy building and provisioning ships and preparing for war. However, when news comes of the earls' defeat in the north, Harold leads his troops on a forced march of about 270 miles all the way to York. And he doesn't waste a moment: on 25 September, at dawn, Harold's crack household warriors, the housecarls, and the rest of his army descend on the unsuspecting Norwegians and, literally, catch them napping. Tostig and Hardrada are slain and it's carnage. They came to England in 300 ships but only twenty-four are needed to take the survivors home again.

But Harold hardly has time to wipe the gore from his sword before news arrives that William of Normandy has made his move at last and landed at Pevensey on the south coast. It's about turn and another forced march back to London to raise more men. One version of the *Anglo-Saxon Chronicle* ends at this point as the scribe can't bear to write the next chapter but we all know how it ends.

'My lord Harold, may I have a word, please?'

'Name of God! I've just beaten Hardrada and that treacherous brother of mine, Tostig, may God have mercy on his wretched soul. That battle at Stamford Bridge was exhausting but my men fought valiantly and Harald Hardrada will get his six feet of English soil, as I promised him when he said he would have every hide of my realm. But barely have I paused for breath and now a messenger tells me that William, the Bastard of Normandy, has landed in Sussex, the impertinent churl. You don't bring me tidings of yet another disaster, do you?'

'No, sire. In fact, I hope to prevent one.'

'Well, I don't have time to dawdle and chat with you. I have hundreds of miles to march; a fresh army to raise. Go and sharpen your sword. Do something useful.'

'It's about your forthcoming fight with William. I have a gift for you. I think you will find it most useful.'

'A gift? Oh well, in that case… What is it? A new battle-axe? My old one has had a lot of use and taken many knocks. A tunic of chain-mail? Could be a life-saver, you know.'

'Better than that, my lord. I've brought you a new helmet. Look here. We call it a motorcycle helmet. It has this brilliant innovation: a transparent visor. You close it down and you can still see everything but it protects your face from, er, falling arrows. You don't want to get an arrow in your eye, do you, my lord? It could be a tragedy for England.'

'Mm. Not of a fashionable design, is it? Whoever wears these mowtasickle helmets? They must look quite foolish with this great dome on their heads. And there's no decoration. Where's the craftsmanship? The gold inlay and enamelling? And not a garnet in sight. I'm the King of England! I need to dress accordingly. Give it to one of my housecarls, though I doubt they'll want it either. Or wear it yourself. You'll look to be a lackwit.'

'But I'll be safe. Are you sure you won't wear it? It would be very advisable. You could glue a few feathers on it.'

'No. I shall wear my own. It's served me well so far and it makes me look like a king… which I am and proud of it.'

'Please, sire.'

'Go away and bother someone else. Find my loyal brothers, Gyrth and Leofwine. I'm sure they'll set you to some useful task, like mucking out the horses.'

'Oh, and a word about those two…'

'Ah, Edith, my love. There you are, dearest. Come with me. It's a fine evening…'

I did try.

A catastrophic end

Another version of the *Anglo-Saxon Chronicle* does tell us about the battle of Hastings in a concise paragraph:

> *King Harold was informed of this* [William's arrival] *and he assembled a large army and came against him at the hoary apple-tree. And William came against him by surprise before his army was drawn up in battle array. But the king nevertheless fought hard against him with the men who were willing to support him and there were heavy casualties on both sides. There King Harold was killed and Earl Leofwine his brother and Earl Gyrth his brother and many good men and the French remained masters of the field.*[2]

King Harold is slain at the Battle of Hastings.

> ### 🔖 Top Tip
>
> In 1066, don't be a thegn of any standing, wealth or significant land-ownership – you'll lose it all to the Normans.

Almost exactly fifty years to the day since Cnut was victorious, thus ends Anglo-Saxon England on 14 Oct 1066 but there will be no return this time. Unlike Cnut who ruled with the co-operation of the English nobles, William will replace them all with his own men. Even the English language disappears from the upper levels of society.

After the battle, Harold's body is so mutilated it can't be easily identified. Only his wife, Edith Swan-neck, knows him intimately enough to say which corpse is that of England's last Anglo-Saxon king.

Conclusion

If you travel back in time to experience Anglo-Saxon England first hand, try to avoid the dates and sites of all those battles, if you want to survive. Don't become too powerful – it can end badly – but keep a low profile. Learn how to make fine jewellery, write manuscripts by hand or become a good storyteller. Knowing how to play the lyre and various board games will make you popular in the mead-hall and earn you a bed for the night. Keep the chapter on the law handy for reference in case someone breaks your finger or hits you on the nose so you'll know how much compensation, *wergild,* you can demand. And whatever you do, don't hit back: you can't afford it.

Otherwise, enjoy your adventure, meet those fascinating people and update history when you return.

Have a safe trip!

Notes

Chapter 1: Introduction

1. Fleming, Robin, *Britain after Rome – The Fall and Rise, 400-1070* [Penguin, 2011], pp.4-5.

Chapter 2: Social Structure

1. https://www.field-studies-council.org/resources/field-studies-journal [accessed April 2023]

Chapter 3: Home and Family

1. Kay, Emma, *Fodder & Drincan – Anglo-Saxon Culinary History* [Prospect Books, 2022], p.153.
2. My thanks to *Regia Anglorum* for this information on the 'Graveney Boat'.
3. www.virologyj.com/content/7/1/52
4. From British Library Manuscripts: Additional 32085 and Royal 12.C.xii. [Hieatt & Jones, *Speculum,* 61/4 [1986], pp.859-882].
5. https://regia.org/research/people/wulfwyn.
6. *Textus Roffensis* https://www.rochestercathedral.org/research/textus/94v-95r
7. Fell, Christine, *Women in Anglo-Saxon England* [British Museum Publications, 1984], p.58.

Chapter 4: Religion – Paganism versus Christianity

1. Fleming, Robin, *Britain after Rome – The Fall and Rise, 400-1070* [Penguin, 2011], pp.120-121.
2. Morris, Marc, *The Anglo-Saxons – A History of the Beginnings of England* [Penguin, 2022], p.54.
3. Kent Archaeological Society Lecture, Canterbury, 21 January 2023.
4. Adams, Max, *The First Kingdom* [Head of Zeus Ltd, 2021], p.374.
5. Fleming, Robin, *Britain after Rome – The Fall and Rise, 400-1070* [Penguin, 2011], p.157.
6. Adams, Max, *The First Kingdom* [Head of Zeus Ltd, 2021], p.424.

Chapter 5: Language and the Law

1. I took this example from 'Teach Yourself Complete Old English (Anglo-Saxon)' by Mark Atherton, 2006.
2. Crystal, David, *The Story of English in 100 Words* [Profile Books, 2011], pp.10-12.
3. http://www.law.harvard.edu/faculty/cdonahue/courses/lhsemelh/materials/Mats2D_2F.pdf
4. Crystal, David, *The Story of English in 100 Words* [Profile Books, 2011], pp.57-58.
5. https://www.bl.uk/collection-items/aelfrics-grammar

Chapter 6: Health and Welfare

1. *The Leechbook of Bald,* British Library, Royal MS 12 DXVII. https://blogs.bl.uk/digitisedmanuscripts/2016/01/balds-leechbook-now-online.html
2. Adams, Max, *In the Land of Giants* [Head of Zeus, 2015], pp.196-98.

Chapter 7: Vikings

1. Cat Jarman, *River Kings – The Vikings from Scandinavia to the Silk Roads* [William Collins, 2021], pp.56-57
2. https://www.thomasnet.com/insights/the-trailblazing-technology-of-viking-ships
3. Cat Jarman, *River Kings – The Vikings from Scandinavia to the Silk Roads* [William Collins, 2021], pp.28-29.
4. Freely adapted from Michael Wood, *In Search of the Dark Ages* [BBC Books, 2022 edition], p.148.

Chapter 8: Arts, Crafts and Literature

1. My thanks go to Gary Payne from 'Here be Flagons' Anglo-Saxon re-enactment group for a demonstration of and information on music, including the 'Trossingen' Anglo-Saxon lyre and the Viking 'tagelharpa' played with a horsehair bow.
2. English Heritage members' lecture given by Dr Matt Thompson via Zoom, 8.11.22
3. Adapted from Magnusson, M., Glover, J. and Mackie, S., *Beowulf* [Alan Sutton Publishing Ltd., 1995]
4. Parker, Eleanor, *Winters in the World – A Journey through the Anglo-Saxon Year* [Reaktion Books, 2022] p.153.
5. *Codex Exoniensis* or Exeter Cathedral Library MS 3501.

Chapter 9: Warfare

1. From Whitehead, Annie, *Women of Power in Anglo-Saxon England,* p.65.
2. Crossley-Holland, Kevin [ed], *The Anglo-Saxon World – An Anthology* [Oxford UP, 2009], pp.11-19.

Chapter 10: The End of the Anglo-Saxon Era

1. Holman, Katherine, *The Northern Conquest: Vikings in Britain and Ireland* [Signal, 2007], p.94.
2. Crossley-Holland, Kevin [ed], *The Anglo-Saxon World – An Anthology* [Oxford UP, 2009], pp.42-43.

List of Illustrations

Front Cover (main image): An Anglo-Saxon king holds court with his Witan or royal council [Hexateuch-Cotton MS Claudius BIV f059r BL] PD

Front Cover (minor images, l to r): A coin of King Eadgar (image 36); Anglo Saxon carving Breedon on the Hill Church (image 1); An amulet or charm will ward of disease and keep you safe; (image 21); Model of St Wystan in St Wystan's Church, Repton, Derbys (image 3)

1. Anglo-Saxon carving of three saints in St Mary & St Hardulph Church, Breedon-on-the-Hill, Leics. [GRM 2023]
2. Lullingstone Roman Villa remains, Kent. Such buildings would be impossible to repair without the right skills and know-how. [GRM 2023]
3. Model of an Anglo-Saxon nobleman, St Wystan, in St Wystan's Church, Repton, Derbys [GRM 2023]
4. The reconstructed Anglo-Saxon weaving-house at West Stow, Suffolk. [GRM 2014]
5. The reconstructed mead-hall at Wychurst, Kent. [GRM 2023, courtesy of *Regia Anglorum*]
6. Interior of the reconstructed mead-hall at Wychurst, Kent. [GRM 2023, courtesy of *Regia Anglorum*]
7. A quern stone being used at Sandwich, Kent, by a member of *Regia Anglorum* [GRM 2023, courtesy of *Regia Anglorum*]
8. Cooking meat on a griddle. [*Regia Anglorum*]
9. The Sutton Hoo cauldron

28. The sword of a Viking buried at Repton [Derby Museum]
29. A reproduction of the Anglo-Saxon 'Trossingen' lyre [GRM 2023, courtesy of Gary Payne of 'Here be Flagons' at Butser, West Sussex.]
30. A reconstruction of the Sutton Hoo helmet [GRM 2023, courtesy of King Penda of Mercia's Court at Butser, West Sussex.]
31. A Sutton Hoo cloisonné shoulder clasp [British Museum, wikicommons, PD]
32. Exquisite Prittlewell glassware made in Kent [GRM 2023, courtesy of Southend-on-Sea Museum, Essex.]
33. Alfred's jewel, the handle of an aestal or pointer for reading text. [Ashmolean Museum, wikicommons, PD]
34. A man playing a 'tagelharpa' [GRM 2023, courtesy of Gary Payne of 'Here be Flagons' at Butser, West Sussex.]
35. Map showing the area of the Danelaw [wikicommons, PD]
36. A coin of King Eadgar [courtesy of Silbury coins]
37. Corfe Castle, scene of King Edward's murder [wikicommons, PD]
38. An Anglo-Saxon shield wall [GRM 2023, courtesy of King Penda of Mercia's Court at Butser, West Sussex.]
39. King Edward the Confessor and Earl Harold Godwineson, Bayeux Tapestry [wikicommons, PD]
40. King Harold is slain at the Battle of Hastings, Bayeux Tapestry [wikicommons, PD]

Acknowledgements

Our thanks go to Southend-on-Sea Museum, Essex, for their kind permission to allow us to take photographs to use as Images 21 and 32 of their Prittlewell Princely Burial Exhibition.

Also to Alan Tidy and Katya Zielonko of *Regia Anglorum* at Wychurst and the re-enactors at Sandwich, Kent [Images 5, 6, 7 and 8], Gary Payne of 'Here be Flagons' at Butser, West Sussex [Images 29 and 34], King Penda of Mercia's Court, Butser, West Sussex [Images 30 and 38], Dartford Museum, Kent [Image 10] and Derby Museum [Image 28].

Bibliography

Original sources

Textus Roffensis, https://www.rochestercathedral.org/research/textus/

Secondary sources

Adams, Max, *In the Land of the Giants* [Head of Zeus Ltd, 2015]

Adams, Max, *Aelfred's Britain* [Head of Zeus Ltd, 2017]

Adams, Max, *The First Kingdom* [Head of Zeus Ltd, 2021]

Atherton, Mark, *Teach Yourself Complete Old English (Anglo-Saxon)* [Hodder Education, 2006]

Barlow, Frank, *The Godwins* [Pearson Education Ltd, 2002]

Brown, Michelle P., *Anglo-Saxon Manuscripts* [The British Library, 1991]

Chown, Vicky & Walker, Kim, *The Handmade Apothecary* [Octopus Publishing, 2017]

Crossley-Holland, Kevin [ed], *The Anglo-Saxon World – An Anthology* [Oxford World's Classics, OUP, 2009 edition]

Crystal, David, *The Story of English in 100 Words* [Profile Books, 2011]

Crystal, D., *The Cambridge Encyclopedia of the English Language* [London, 1995]

Evans, Angela Care, *The Sutton Hoo Ship Burial* [British Museum Press, 2002 ed.]

Fleming, Robin, *Britain after Rome – The Fall and Rise, 400-1070* [Penguin Books, 2011]

Fell, Christine, *Women in Anglo-Saxon England* [British Museum Publications, 1984]

Gross, M.W. & D. McKenna, *Old English Literature* [London, 1973]

Henson, Donald, *A Guide to Late Anglo-Saxon England – From Aelfred to Eadgar II* [Anglo-Saxon Books, 1998]

Herbert, Kathleen, *Peace-Weavers & Shield Maidens – Women in Early English Society* [Anglo-Saxon Books, 1997]

Higham, Nicholas J., *The Death of Anglo-Saxon England* [Sutton Publishing Ltd. 1997]

Hirst, S. & Scull, C., *The Anglo-Saxon Princely Burial at Prittlewell, Southend-on-Sea* [MOLA, 2019]

Jarman, Cat, *River Kings – The Vikings from Scandinavia to the Silk Roads* [William Collins, 2021]

Kay, Emma, *Fodder & Drincan – Anglo-Saxon Culinary History* [Prospect Books, 2022]

Kuhn, Sherman M., *Studies in the Language and Poetics of Anglo-Saxon England* [Ann Arbor, 1984]

Magnusson, M., Glover, J. and Mackie, S., *Beowulf* [Alan Sutton Publishing Ltd., 1995]

Morris, Marc, *The Anglo-Saxons – A History of the Beginnings of England* [Penguin, 2022]

Mount, Toni, *Everyday Life in Medieval London – From the Anglo-Saxons to the Tudors* [Amberley, 2014]

Parker, Eleanor, *Winters in the World – A Journey through the Anglo-Saxon Year* [Reaktion Books, 2022]

Scott, K.L. *Dated and Datable English Manuscript Borders c. 1395-1499* [London, 2002]

Storr, Jim, *King Arthur's Wars: The Anglo-Saxon Conquest of England* [Solihull, 2016]

Whitehead, Annie, *Women of Power in Anglo-Saxon England* [Pen & Sword History, 2022]

Williams, Thomas, *Viking Britain* [Collins, 2017]

Williams, Thomas, *Viking London* [Collins, 2020]

Wood, Michael, *In Search of the Dark Ages* [BBC Books, 2022 updated edition]

Index